SYSTEMIC RISKS IN SECURITIES MARKETS

ORGANISATION FOR ECONOMIC CO-OPERATION AND DEVELOPMENT

Pursuant to Article 1 of the Convention signed in Paris on 14th December 1960, and which came into force on 30th September 1961, the Organisation for Economic Co-operation and Development (OECD) shall promote policies designed:

- to achieve the highest sustainable economic growth and employment and a rising standard of living in Member countries, while maintaining financial stability, and thus to contribute to the development of the world economy;
- to contribute to sound economic expansion in Member as well as non-member countries in the process of economic development; and
- to contribute to the expansion of world trade on a multilateral, non-discriminatory basis in accordance with international obligations.

The original Member countries of the OECD are Austria, Belgium, Canada, Denmark, France, Germany, Greece, Iceland, Ireland, Italy, Luxembourg, the Netherlands, Norway, Portugal, Spain, Sweden, Switzerland, Turkey, the United Kingdom and the United States. The following countries became Members subsequently through accession at the dates indicated hereafter: Japan (28th April 1964), Finland (28th January 1969), Australia (7th June 1971) and New Zealand (29th May 1973). The Commission of the European Communities takes part in the work of the OECD (Article 13 of the OECD Convention). Yugoslavia takes part in some of the work of the OECD (agreement of 28th October 1961).

Publié en français sous le titre :

**RISQUES SYSTÉMIQUES
DANS LES MARCHÉS
DES VALEURS MOBILIÈRES**

Reprinted, 1992

This report represents a response by the Committee on Financial Markets to the concerns regarding the stability and safety of the international financial system which the OECD Council at Ministerial level expressed in its communiqué of 19 May 1988 as follows:

> "The Organisation will intensify its efforts to analyse the nature and functioning of the emerging global financial system and to identify gaps and inadequacies in the coverage and co-ordination of prudential arrangements, especially in the case of securities markets".

At its meeting held on 9-10 November 1988, the Committee on Financial Markets set up an Ad Hoc Group of Experts on Securities Markets under the chairmanship of Mr. M.E. Hewitt of the Bank of England to deal with this Ministerial mandate and focus in particular on issues pertaining to systemic risks in securities markets. The Committee approved the report, which the Expert Group prepared with active participation in particular by its chairman, at its meeting held on 30-31 October 1990. The OECD Council agreed to the publication of the report on 7 December 1990.

Also available

"Trends in Banking Structure and Regulation in OECD Countries" Series:

Competition in Banking (1989)
(21 89 01 1) ISBN 92-64-13197-3 FF195 £ 23.50 US$41.00 DM80

Prudential Supervision in Banking *by R.M. Pecchioli* (1987)
(21 87 03 1) ISBN 92-64-12916-2 FF130 £ 13.00 US$26.00 DM58

Trends in Banking in OECD Countries (1985)
(21 85 04 1) ISBN 92-64-12762-3 FF60 £ 6.00 US$12.00 DM27

Financial Market Trends:

No. 44 (1989)
(27 89 03 1) FF80 £10.00 US$17.00 DM33

No. 46 (1990)
(27 90 02 1) FF80 £10.00 US$17.00 DM33

Prices charged at the OECD Bookshop.

THE OECD CATALOGUE OF PUBLICATIONS and supplements will be sent free of charge on request addressed either to OECD Publications Service, 2, rue André-Pascal, 75775 PARIS CEDEX 16, or to the OECD Distributor in your country.

TABLE OF CONTENTS

SYSTEMIC RISKS IN SECURITIES MARKETS

A. Introduction and terms of reference

1. At its meeting in November 1988 the Committee on Financial Markets set up an ad hoc group of experts on securities markets, whose members are listed in Annex 1, under the chairmanship of Mr. M.E. Hewitt of the Bank of England with the following terms of reference.

2. a) Against the background of the structural changes under way in securities markets, to identify the risks inherent in those markets and to assess their importance from an overall systemic risk point of view, distinguishing between risks at the level of different types of financial intermediaries, on the one hand, and risks arising from market structures and settlement systems, on the other;

b) To review the principles underlying and changes taking place in regulatory arrangements in OECD Member countries designed to contain the risks analysed under point a) above and to follow progress in discussions on these matters in other fora;

c) To assess implications for prudential arrangements in OECD Member countries arising from the internationalisation of financial markets, notably securities markets. The following aspects should receive special attention:

- Compatibility of national prudential arrangements inside the OECD area and in major non-OECD financial centres;

- Risk management of securities business by internationally-operating banks and securities firms;

- Assessment of the scope for international chain effects from crises in national financial systems ("contagion effect").

3. These terms of reference can be put more concisely as to assess the risks arising from structural changes in world securities markets which might lead to a damaging disruption of those markets and the international financial system of which they are an important part; and to review the scope for improving the capacity of the system to manage those risks.

4. As the terms of reference require, this report focuses on securities markets, which are taken to mean equity, bond and derivative markets. But major crises in these markets cannot necessarily be contained within them because the main operators in them are also large operators in foreign exchange and money markets, and because major failures also affect the payments and banking systems. Similarly, movements in foreign exchange or money markets may lead to or coincide with movements in securities markets, and bank failures or payments breakdowns could disrupt securities markets. This nexus of potential interrelationships has to be constantly borne in mind.

5. The main focus of the report is on those features of market structure and regulation which increase (or fail to reduce) the risk of an international financial crisis occurring, or aggravate it once started, and on the scope for reforms to reduce the vulnerability of the system. It discusses only cursorily the macroeconomic causes and effects of crises in securities markets. Where the causes are not structural to the market, they are regarded as given, exogenous shocks which test the resilience of the system but are beyond the power of market participants and regulators to prevent (though not necessarily to anticipate). The real macroeconomic effects of financial crises are outside the scope of this study, but the assumption is made that failure to contain a major international financial crisis could have damaging enough real effects to justify action to strengthen the capacity of the system to withstand shocks.

6. Containment of a crisis may in most cases depend more on the actions of the monetary authorities than on those of market or institutional regulators. In making such interventions the monetary authorities may be diverted from their chosen path in pursuing their main function of safeguarding the stability of the currency; if they decide to give direct financial support to intermediaries in difficulty they put public funds at risk; and expectations that they will intervene may encourage intermediaries to take excessive risks. These considerations give the monetary authorities a powerful interest in the development of market structures and regulatory arrangements which minimise the need for intervention on their part. So the main emphasis in this report is on ex ante preventative rather than ex post remedial measures.

B. Interdependence and volatility of securities markets

7. There have been huge changes in world capital markets over the last decade, which have not yet run their full course. These are so familiar that there is no need to do more than rehearse them briefly in this report. In combination they have increased the degree of interdependence between national financial markets.

8. First, the abolition of exchange controls, the breaking down of entry barriers to national markets, including those preventing foreign or institutional ownership of securities dealers, the unfixing of commission rates in the United States, United Kingdom and other markets and relaxations of other restrictions (such as those on foreign investment by pension funds) have removed major legal and institutional obstacles to cross-border capital flows.

9. In these conditions of greater freedom large institutional investors seeking to diversify their portfolios and large industrial and commercial companies searching for the best terms on which to finance their own multinational operations have looked for opportunities outside as well as inside their domestic financial markets. The amount of funds which the former have to invest and the latter need to finance their operations have both been growing rapidly. Long-term financial institutions such as pension funds have, moreover, been increasing their share of savings in the United States, the United Kingdom and Japan.

10. In consequence, there has been an expansion in international bond markets, especially the euro-bond market; in cross-border investment in national bond and equity markets; and, albeit on a less dramatic scale, in international equity issues. There has also been a striking growth in the invention and use of new instruments such as swaps, financial futures and options, which have increased the ability of users of financial markets to cope with fluctuations in exchange rates, interest rates and security prices. Futures and options have increased the opportunity for hedging and arbitrage between cash and derivative markets; and thus made those markets interdependent nationally and, in some contracts, internationally. Swaps have enabled lenders and borrowers with different preferences as between currencies or as between fixed and floating rate interest payments or receipts to find the terms which they consider the most suitable for them by exchanging obligations with counterparties with complementary preferences. In so doing they have acted as a force integrating securities markets internationally. At the same time there is always a

degree of risk when new financial instruments are developed that unfamiliarity may lead to imprudent use: and it does not necessarily follow that every new financial instrument increases the efficiency of capital markets and the real economy.

11. The main sources of innovation, and the main intermediaries in this process of the internationalisation and securitisation of capital markets have been large, internationally active American, Japanese and European banks (including the securities subsidiaries of United Kingdom and French banks) and, especially, the large American and Japanese non-bank securities houses. It is these institutions which have taken on the sizeable position-taking commitments as market makers or underwriters in bond, equity, futures, options, swaps and other markets, including short-term money and foreign exchange markets, which have made an orderly, efficient flow of capital between final users possible on such a large scale.

12. Those intermediaries have themselves been subject to the forces of competition and change as well as its agents. In particular, the Big Bang changes in London led to the formation of new financial conglomerates as banks became the owners of securities dealers. Because of its openness London was also the financial centre where American and Japanese banks and securities houses, legally separated by Glass-Steagall and Article 65, were able, respectively, to conduct securities or banking transactions which were not permitted in their own countries. These developments increased the number of leading financial intermediaries conducting both banking and securities operations, and thus, in the case of the banks concerned, their direct exposure to position risks in securities on their own balance sheets or through subsidiaries as well as their indirect exposure through their credit and trading relationships with securities houses in a range of markets. These developments were, of course, less novel in universal banking systems.

13. Finally technological advances in communications have accelerated the international flow of information to markets. The ability to transmit news virtually instantly throughout the major markets of the world, even though subject to the natural constraints imposed by time zone differences, has increased the speed of market response to such news. Improved technology has also driven down the cost of operation, thereby permitting in part the use of certain hedging strategies. Moreover, the development of electronic trading systems appears likely to increase the scope for 24-hour, cross-border trading in the coming decade. The forerunner in this respect is likely to be the Globex system for after-hours electronic trading in futures being developed by the Chicago Mercantile Exchange and by Reuters, which will potentially embrace the contracts of other futures exchanges around the world. Separate plans have also recently been announced by the New York Stock Exchange, by NASDAQ International, and, in conjunction with Reuters, by three other United States exchanges (the American Stock Exchange, the Chicago Board Options Exchange, and the Cincinatti Stock Exchange) to introduce after-hours electronic trading in equities and (in the last-named case) in equity options.

14. The thrust of most of these developments has been overwhelmingly beneficial in making capital markets freer, more competitive and more efficient, and increasing the flow of international capital. But the very fact that they have increased the extent of integration between national markets has increased the likelihood that markets around the world will move in similar directions. Studies [e.g. by Dimson and Marsh of the London Business School (1) and Bertero and Mayer of the City University Business School in London (2)] have indeed shown a greater correlation between movements in prices on major national equity markets developing in the eighties, and, although this is a short period on which to base very firm conclusions, the study by Bertero and Mayer also shows an increase in such correlation in the period following the October 1987 crash (on top, of course, of the very marked correlation during the crash itself). Other studies [e.g. by Neumark, Tinsley and Tosini (3) in the United States and by King, Sentana and Wadwhani (4) in the United Kingdom] suggest that positive price correlations among major national equity markets are most apparent during periods of sharp price movements. Moreover, the plunge in share prices on 13 October 1989, its replication in European markets on 16 October, and the subsequent recovery led

by Wall Street in the afternoon of 16 October (European time) again vividly demonstrated the transmission of a sharp market movement from one time zone to another (although the fall on Tokyo was much lower). On the other hand the sharp falls in share prices in Tokyo in the first few months of 1990 have not been echoed to the same extent in other markets.

15. Dimson and Marsh observed stronger correlations between movements in indices for the leading quoted companies than those for smaller companies, suggesting that since such companies are the most dependent for their success on international trading they will be perceived to be similarly affected by major pieces of international economic news, whatever the comparative performance or cyclical stage of their national economies. Similarly Bertero and Mayer found strongest correlations between movements in equity markets with the highest proportion of commonly traded shares -- which is perhaps not surprising.

16. Using conventional measures, these and other studies have not so far found there to have been any increase in the volatility of equity prices -- omitting, however, from consideration the immediate few days of the crash itself -- either in the period before the crash or the period following it. For example, in the United States, the average daily standard deviation of returns on New York Stock Exchange stocks exhibited no statistically significant trend in the 1980s. One measure, however, which does suggest that volatility increased over the decade is the frequency of extreme daily price movements. In particular the 1980s experienced a higher frequency of abnormally large daily movements in returns to the Standard and Poor Composite Index, with twenty of the fifty largest post-war daily percentage movements occurring in this decade, and fifteen of those after 1985, as has been pointed out in a Federal Reserve Board staff paper by Duffee, Kupiec and White (5). In an article on measuring financial market volatility Becketti and Sellon of the Federal Reserve Bank of Kansas City (6) confirm this finding of an increase in what they term jump volatility in the eighties. In the same article they find that the volatility of returns on long-term United States Treasury Bonds has also increased in the eighties, and that exchange rate volatility in the same period has been generally higher than in the early years of floating exchange rates after 1973.

17. The evidence of increased interdependence between national markets, especially in periods of large price movements, and the greater frequency of such movements, appear more significant than the lack of evidence of generally increased volatility in equity markets. Moreover, as the October 1989 experience reminds us, the latter tells us little about the probability of precipitous collapses of the October 1987 kind recurring. It would seem rash to rule out the possibility of another sharp downward adjustment in prices -- on equity and/or bond markets -- which ran rapidly from one national market to another. If there were a crisis, it would be liable to spread quickly.

18. The discussion on this section of the paper has focused so far on major developments which have acted to increase not only the free flow of capital but also, on the whole, the efficient functioning of capital markets internationally. But the experience of October 1987 revealed some respects in which discontinuities and inefficiencies in the working of markets exacerbated or threatened to exacerbate the crisis.

19. As the Brady Report (7) pointed out, the 1987 crisis in the United States revealed capacity failures of systems to handle the unprecedented volume of selling orders, disconnections between the securities market in New York and the index futures and options markets in Chicago, and vulnerabilities and inefficiencies in clearing and settlement systems. Similar problems with capacity constraints and settlement systems were observed in other countries as well. Since then several exchanges, clearing houses and self-regulatory organisations have initiated improvements. For example, the United States securities, futures and options exchanges have taken various measures to increase order-handling capacity and to co-operate among themselves, including an agreement to impose co-ordinated trading halts when the market falls by a pre-agreed number of points. The questions about market mechanisms which arise are discussed in Section E. There has also been a general recognition of the need to improve the functioning of

settlement systems and to work towards common national standards, as evidenced in the reports of the Group of Thirty and the Fédération Internationale des Bourses de Valeurs (FIBV) on this subject. These issues are discussed in Section F of the report.

C. Features of financial crises in securities markets

20. This report was commissioned by the OECD in the aftermath of the collapse in world equity prices in October 1987 -- the most obvious recent example of a crisis which appeared to pose a systemic threat. To the extent that there are lessons to be learnt from that experience or questions still to be resolved they must form the basis of much of the analysis in this report. The October 1987 experience also stimulated more intense academic discussion of the theory of financial crisis. It may be worthwhile at this point to consider some of the fruits of that discussion, and some of the other international financial crises which provided the material for study, to see if some common strands can be drawn from them.

21. For this purpose a convenient and recent analytical work is a paper by Mr. E.P. Davis on "Instability in the euro-markets and the economic theory of financial crisis" (Bank of England Discussion Paper No. 43 of October 1989) (8). This assesses four periods of financial disorder in the euro-markets in the light of various theoretical approaches proposed in the academic literature. The periods assessed were 1974 (Herstatt), 1982 (Debt Crisis), 1986 [Floating Rate Note (FRN) Market] and 1987 (Equity Market). Comparative analysis revealed that these periods of financial instability had many features in common. It did not give overwhelming support to any one theory of crisis but suggested the need for a selective synthesis of them.

22. This study is particularly relevant to the purposes of the present report because it looks at experience in the euro-markets, the most international of securities markets. At the same time this encompasses the market in syndicated bank loans, and refers almost entirely to debt rather than equity markets. To that extent its emphasis differs from the present report which is more, though not exclusively, concerned with the potential for international crises in equity markets. For this reason the following is in part a summary of Davis' conclusions on the common features of financial fragility in the euro-markets in the period of 1984-87 and in part an interpretation of them based on this different emphasis. Hence it may in the process vary from his own interpretation.

23. The following were the common features which, with varying degrees of strength, Davis found as a result of his study; brief interpretative comments with the bias described above follow each of his eight conclusions.

i) **They followed accumulation of debt and substantial accumulation of assets which were often characterised by crowd-like behaviour among lenders, low risk premia and concentration of risk.** This is consistent with those economic theories which emphasise excessive debt accumulation and fragility as causes of crisis. Accumulation of debt prior to the crisis was more marked in the first three episodes (inter-bank positions prior to 1974, third world debt prior to 1982, and FRNs in 1986) than in the period preceding October 1987 (although there had been strong growth in United States corporate debt and a reduction in margins on syndicated corporate credits in the euro-markets). Large underwriting positions added to market problems in the 1987 crash. In particular, the United Kingdom Government's international sale of BP shares left a few United States underwriters heavily exposed, caught by an unfortunate combination of United Kingdom requirements for a long exposure time and United States requirements under which they could not unload their holdings in advance of the issue. The actual losses generated for these and other underwriters and, still more, the knowledge of their existence overhanging the market had a depressing effect both on market prices generally and on confidence in the institutions known to be holding large positions. The subsequent decision by the United Kingdom authorities to buy back the shares when they reached a stated floor price did much to restore stability.

ii) **They followed a shift of régime which had unforeseeable or unforeseen consequences.** This is consistent with theories on the role of uncertainty in crises (as also are evidence of crowd psychology and competitive innovation). The first two episodes, however, provide clearer evidence of this, in the shift from fixed to floating exchange rates prior to 1974 and in the second oil shock, major recession and changes in United States monetary policy prior to 1982, than do the latter two episodes. In 1986 the failure was rather more to appreciate the dynamics of a market in existing, though relatively new instruments. Whether there was any sufficiently fundamental change in the environment prior to October 1987 to be described as a change in régime also seems doubtful, (although it was a period in which the structural developments on international securities markets described in Section B were gathering momentum and in which use of techniques of dynamic hedging became more widespread). Moreover, as Davis points out, proponents of the uncertainty theory and others who put emphasis on the human tendency towards "disaster myopia" can point out that, since there had been no experience of a major stock market collapse for so long, there was a collective, self-deluding failure to attach more than a low probability to the prospect of a collapse of the size and abruptness of that which occurred. Reliance on portfolio insurance programmes probably contributed to this.

iii) **Innovation was often an important concomitant, as were declining capital ratios of lenders and borrowers.** These are really two separate features. The first is most consistent with uncertainty theories, the second with financial fragility and credit rationing theories. Innovation was a feature of the three crises in the 1980s. In the debt crisis the syndicated bank credit was the main innovation together with sovereign lending itself. The FRN market was characterised by a wide variety of innovations which attempted to compensate for declining spreads. The 1987 equity market crisis followed innovations such as portfolio insurance, but these appear to have been an exacerbating rather than a causal factor. Declining capital ratios were evident for banks prior to the 1974 and 1982 crises but, owing to pressure from supervisors, commercial banks had a much stronger position in 1986 and 1987. On the other hand there was concern in 1987 (albeit exaggerated) over the capital strength of some United States investment banks with large underwriting or other positions in equities, and over the heavy indebtedness of some United States corporations. Somewhat similar concerns associated with the financing of leveraged buy-outs surfaced in October 1989.

iv) **They often followed a period of monetary tightening (necessitated by inflationary pressures) and/or recession.** This gives partial credence to a monetarist approach which identifies financial crises with banking panics which may either lead to monetary contraction or worsen the macroeconomic effects of prior contraction: and whose policy prescriptions consequently are for a stable and predictable path for the money supply, and a readiness by the authorities to expand the money supply at times of financial crises. Real United States monetary growth was low or declining prior to the 1974, 1982 and 1987 crises (but rapid in the year before the FRN crisis), suggesting a degree of restraint by the monetary authorities (following earlier relaxation). The 1974 and 1982 crises also occurred after cyclical peaks in activity. The crises do not appear, however, to have caused a reduction in the money supply. Nor were banking panics a feature of most of the episodes, although the 1974 Herstatt crisis showed some of the signs of one. This may partly be attributed, particularly in 1982 and 1987, to central bank intervention; by the same token, relaxations of monetary policy on these occasions helped to offset any tendency for monetary contraction.

v) **They were accompanied by sharp increases in price and quantity rationing of credit, but this did not always prevent rationed borrowers from obtaining credit elsewhere.** This is most consistent with theories which associate financial crises with decisions to ration credit following an earlier period of excessive, indiscriminate credit expansion (and which build on the financial fragility and uncertainty theories). Some degree of credit rationing was a widely observed feature during or after all of the crises. In the two most recent episodes, which are also the clearer examples of crises originating in securities markets rather than in banking activity, the FRN market virtually closed for new issues in 1986 as did the equity warrant euro-bond sector in 1987, and only top quality borrowers could gain access to the straight euro-bond sector. It can be added that in the first part of 1988 there was also a marked reduction in the number and size of equity issues on several major domestic markets. In 1987, too, securities houses with equity exposures initially faced the threat of rationing of bank credit. Had this threat been realised the potential systemic repercussions would have increased, but in the event banks refrained from calling loans to securities firms and increased credit outstanding. Nevertheless, neither crisis had long-lasting effects on the ability of companies, banks or financial institutions to raise finance, but rather shifted it temporarily to different sources.

vi) **International transmission was strong and rapid.** This is consistent with several theories. Because the subject of the Davis study was the international euro-markets, which were involved in or affected by all four episodes, the effects were self-evidently not confined to one national market. The 1987 equity market crash provides the clearest case of all of a rapid transmission of a sharp fall in security prices around the world, starting in this case, however, in a national market. The fall in prices on Wall Street on 19 and 20 October 1987 led a sequence of falls on Pacific and European equity markets and related futures and options markets, running consecutively from one time zone to the next (although the falls varied in size on different national markets). A similar, though shorter-lived and less precipitous, sequence was triggered by the fall on Wall Street on 13 October 1989 and in the reverse direction by the recovery on 16 October 1989 (although price movements in Tokyo were much smaller than elsewhere).

vii) **Contagion between euro-markets was limited -- in no case were all euro-markets strongly affected.** In 1974 the crisis in the interbank market had repercussions in the credits market, but fixed-rate bond issues remained buoyant. In 1982 the prolonged fall in credits was accompanied by an increase in fixed-rate bond issues and inter-bank lending and a fall in FRNs in the initial quarter of the crisis, but by a year later only fixed-rate bond issues had increased. The crisis in the FRN market was largely confined to that market. In October 1987 there was some initial contagion from the domestic equity markets to the euro-bond market where activity fell sharply and margins over government issues widened, but contagion to other euro-markets was more muted, and there was some flight to quality to domestic government bond markets. Activity in euro-credits increased sharply, however, in the initial quarter and continued to rise in the following year when euro-bond issues also revived.

viii) **Decisive action by the authorities prevented the crisis from having serious systemic and macroeconomic consequences.** Most theories highlight this as the immediate solution to financial crises when they occur: these are not felt to be events that the market can sort out painlessly by itself. Intervention by the United States Federal Reserve System and other central banks was most evident in the 1987 equity market crash but was also apparent in the debt crisis and the 1974 episode. The FRN crisis was more localised and was allowed to blow itself out.

24. This review of the common features of the four crises suggests that the preconditions for a financial crisis typically include intense market competition in new instruments leading to underpricing of risk premia and concentrations in relatively high-risk assets. Both supervisors and market participants need to monitor and guard against these trends. If they occur in expansionary monetary conditions, securities prices generally may become over-inflated; necessary corrective action by the monetary authorities could in such conditions be one factor which might trigger a sharp devaluation. This reinforces the general case for sound and steady monetary policies. When there is such a sharp readjustment of securities prices of the kind considered here, however triggered, it may but will not necessarily spread from one country to another and from one market to another. The monetary authorities may then need to intervene through the provision of liquidity to the system or, in some cases, by the provision or organisation of more direct financial support to prevent the spread of further damage to the financial system and the real economy. At the same time, in order to preserve flexibility and to reduce the moral hazard of underwriting imprudent behaviour by intermediaries, there is a strong case to be made against setting precise contingency plans as to when, where and to what extent, if at all, the authorities could be expected to intervene.

D. Systemic risks and systemic crisis

25. Against the background of the structural developments discussed in Section B and the features of four financial crises discussed in Section C, this section discusses what is meant in this report by systemic risks and systemic crisis; and considers how such a crisis could develop.

26. Any system is a set of interrelated parts which recognisably constitute a connected whole. In that sense any financial market is a system the components of which are its trading and regulatory arrangements and the participants in the market. This report is concerned with the interactions between several layers of systems. The first layer consists of national securities markets, the second the system of international securities markets of which they are a part, the third the international financial system of which they in turn are a part, and the fourth the world economy of which that is a part.

27. A systemic crisis is a disturbance which severely impairs the working of the system; and at the extreme causes a complete breakdown in it. Systemic risks are those risks which have the potential to cause such a crisis and, at the extreme, such a breakdown in the system. It is possible to advance more precise definitions. For instance one member of the ad hoc group, Mr. Sean O'Connor of the Bank of Canada, in a perceptive paper entitled "Systemic Risks in Securities Markets: A Concept in Search of a Definition" (9) has concluded that "systemic risk is the financial risk that arises from institutional and structural arrangements in markets which all participants (in the economy) must bear as a group". This definition is illuminating in directing attention to faults or inconsistencies in institutional and structural arrangements -- which is indeed the central subject for attention in this report.

28. Thus, conceptually, discussion in this report could embrace the transmission of shocks from bottom to top or from top to bottom of the four layers of system mentioned. In practice our main concern is with the transmission of shocks from international securities markets or large domestic markets to the international financial system. Thus we are interested in the bottom layer of national securities markets primarily as components of the international system and in the extent to which a crisis in one national market might spread to others.

29. So far as the top layer is concerned, the assumption has already been mentioned in paragraph 5 that a grave enough financial crisis could do damage to the real economy. A breakdown in capital markets would disrupt the process of saving and investment and undermine the long-term confidence of private investors: a breakdown of the banking and payments systems as a consequence of a collapse of securities markets would disrupt the normal course of economic transactions which they facilitate. The extent of the damage would clearly depend on the size and the duration of the breakdown, as well as on the readiness and ability of the monetary and other appropriate authorities to take corrective action.

30. Recent experience has in some respects been encouraging from this point of view. Action by the Federal Reserve Board and by other central banks was almost certainly critical in arresting the market fall of October 1987 and confidence that there would be similar action if necessary may possibly have been an important factor in arresting the fall in October 1989. The real economic consequences of the October 1987 crash appear to have been minimal: the world economy resumed its trend of strong growth in 1988. Arguably the main consequence for the real economy was that the relaxation of monetary policy in response to the crash strengthened inflationary pressures. It may remain possible, however, that if a fall in stock prices such as that in October 1987 were to occur at a time when the business cycle was entering the downswing, then it might provoke a faster and steeper fall in activity.

31. In the securities markets there was a dampening effect both on new issues and on secondary market turnover throughout most of 1988. Nevertheless major equity markets regained buoyancy in 1989 which was only temporarily interrupted by the plunge in prices on 13-16 October. In the securities industry itself there has been an appreciable shakeout in activity and employment among intermediaries, but this may be seen as a salutary correction of an earlier state of hyper-activity and over-capacity. Market makers have taken a more cautious attitude to holding large positions but it is unclear whether this amounts to a major or lasting impairment in market liquidity.

32. Again, this report does not attempt to analyse the effect which news of real economic events has on securities markets. Securities markets do react continually to economic information, and a major change in economic direction is likely to be reflected in (or sometimes anticipated by) movements in securities prices. A large and sudden economic shock may be expected to precipitate a corresponding market response. It would probably be futile to try to predict what form such a shock might take. Perhaps, however, it would not take so great a shock to produce a large market response in a situation where confidence was already sensitive as a result of weaknesses or disequilibria in the real economy. For instance, persistent imbalances in current account payments between major economies may leave securities markets more than normally inclined to react abruptly to unfavourable developments or to policy responses by governments perceived to be inadequate.

33. We cannot, moreover, be so confident of our understanding of either the causes or the consequences of sudden collapses in securities markets as to rule out the possibility that similar episodes will not recur or that, when they do, they will not develop far enough to wreak real economic damage. That uncertainty makes it the more important to examine the characteristics of such crises and the systemic risks and stresses which they expose or exacerbate.

34. The extreme systemic threat arising from a collapse of securities prices is that default by one or more large securities dealers will lead to further defaults and that the failures will extend into the core of the banking system and cause a breakdown in the flow of payments in settlement of financial transactions throughout the world. This threat did not become reality in October 1987. No significant failures occurred in major financial centres other than Hong Kong. Wall Street turned in time to pull itself back from the brink, and other markets followed, but the experience provided some indications of how such a catastrophic sequence might start, and then accelerate once started.

35. One dangerous possibility raised was that the sequence could start with a withdrawal of funding rather than actual insolvency. This is because in a situation of general panic, creditors and counterparties will grow most alarmed at their exposure to those institutions which they believe to be the least able to absorb large losses on their positions. This may lead banks to ask for increased collateral on loans at a time when the asset value of that collateral is falling, or to withdraw credit lines entirely. Futhermore counterparties may cease trading with the institutions concerned. In such circumstances a firm facing a funding problem may be forced into insolvency; and, if that happens, it could trigger further defaults and lead to the failure of other firms.

36. This possibility is inherent in the nature and scale of the funding and trading interrelationships between large securities houses and between them and their bankers over a variety of markets in different instruments, currencies and time zones. Large securities houses borrow large amounts of funds in the course of their business. Since these are predominantly wholesale funds borrowed at short-term in the money market, they are arguably more vulnerable to a loss of confidence than are banks funded by a large retail deposit base supported by deposit insurance and presumed access to a lender of last resort. (Many banks, of course, are also dependent upon inter-bank and other short-term wholesale funding for a large part of their liabilities which could disappear quickly in a crisis). Moreover since the financing needs of securities traders shift so rapidly from one minute to the next as their positions fluctuate, their relationships with their creditors need to be and typically are correspondingly flexible. They will move rapidly between several sources of finance in search of the lowest interest rates. In these conditions a creditor may not know at any one time the extent of his exposure to a particular institution. This difficulty is compounded by the degree of exposure that major securities houses will have with each other and with leading banks in forward as well as cash markets, and in overseas as well as domestic markets. It may well be impossible to calculate, at least intra-day, the total exposure which one firm may have to another over all markets; even more critically, it will be impossible for each firm to estimate the exposures of its counterparties to others. In a crisis this ignorance about the full extent of exposure to individual institutions itself generates anxiety and may lead lenders and fellow traders to assume the worst about the institutions perceived to be in the weakest state.

37. If particular institutions do face funding problems they will need to resort to sales of assets. But this will add to the downward pressure on securities prices in the market and on the value of the firm's remaining holdings. Or they may have holdings of relatively unmarketable securities which they cannot sell in time. Although the net liquid assets requirements imposed by securities regulators such as those in the United States, United Kingdom and Japan are designed to cope with such situations, securities classified as liquid may well become distinctly less marketable in a crisis. It is not hard to see how in these conditions an illiquid firm could become insolvent; and, precisely because of the network of credit and trading relationships with other market participants, failure of one major firm in these circumstances cannot be guaranteed to be an isolated case.

38. Such a crisis also tests the efficiency and robustness of settlement systems. This applies both to the centralised clearing and guarantee systems used in futures and options markets, and to the diverse array of settlement arrangements in cash securities markets. There were several instances in October 1987 which demonstrated the key role of such systems. The extreme case was the rescue operation which had to be launched for the inadequately capitalised Hong Kong Futures Guarantee Corporation. But in the United States the near failure of the largest clearing member of the Options Clearing Corporation, as a result of large defaults by its customers, was also a worrying event which, without the injection of capital from its bank holding company parent, might have triggered defaults by other clearing firms and put extreme pressure on the capacity of the clearing corporation to meet its obligations. Late payment of large margin transfers by the Chicago Mercantile Exchange's Clearing Division also stimulated some short-lived concern. Although they did not develop further, these incidents suggested how concern about the viability of a clearing house could undermine confidence in the market which it cleared, and lead to a rush by

customers and dealers to close positions. Disorderly conditions in a derivative market would in turn be likely to spill over into the underlying cash market. Firms with long cash positions hedged by short positions on the futures or options market would fear that the protection these gave would disappear, and decide to take their losses by selling on the cash market, thus adding to the downward pressures on prices.

39. While in London no significant failures occurred on the futures, options or cash markets, the length of the settlement period on the equity market (effectively three weeks), together with the large accumulated backlog of unsettled transactions left over from previous settlement periods, did increase the degree of uncertainty about the extent of credit and trading exposures of individual firms. In the event these did not cause banks to withhold credit from securities firms, even where their normal limits were exceeded. Nevertheless the delay before this could be established was a confidence weakening factor.

40. A further point to be made in this part of the discussion is the obvious one that because some of the main American securities houses are prominent dealers in securities markets outside the United States, their failure could have an international as well as domestic impact. This also applies, but for the most part to a lesser extent, to institutions from other countries which operate internationally. Other countries besides the home country thus have an interest that the managements of such groups keep track of their worldwide operations and provide for their total risk exposure; and that their home supervisory authorities are able to exercise adequate oversight over them. This is by no means always the case at present. Gaps in supervisory coverage are considered further in Section G.

41. Recapitulation of the stages by which the processes described in the preceding paragraphs could lead to a systemic crisis may be helpful in identifying the critical elements in the process. First, the sequence starts with a sharp and sudden fall in prices of securities or derivatives. Second, this spreads rapidly to other securities markets. Third, this leads to the failure of one or more major intermediaries. Fourth, this generates a crisis in the core banking and payments system.

42. To set such a sequence of events in motion, the initial fall in prices must almost certainly occur in a major national market or in the euro-markets. Both the 1987 and 1989 episodes began in the United States markets, and this remains a potential source. But a disturbance in the euro-markets or a few other major markets such as Tokyo or London might also act as a catalyst, although, of course, this would depend very much on investor reactions and other local factors. For example, share price movements were not as pronounced in Tokyo in October 1989 as in other countries; and although there have been some unusually sharp price falls in Tokyo in the first few months of 1990 which have contributed to nervousness in international markets they have not led to comparable price movements in the United States and in Europe. (This refers to price falls before those set off by the Middle Eastern crisis in August.) Investors took an essentially local view of the causes of the initial fall in prices, although this may not always be the case when a sudden price fall occurs in this or another major market. A sharp price fall on one of the next most important group of national securities markets such as Frankfurt, or Paris, or Toronto, or Sydney, or Switzerland, or Hong Kong might conceivably also have a significant international impact; but such a fall would be more likely to be seen as reflecting local developments.

43. A market crisis spread over many and major national securities markets is probably itself a necessary condition for a liquidity or solvency failure of one or more major internationally active financial intermediaries of a kind which would endanger the system. Although a single such intermediary might fail in other circumstances as a result of wrong decisions by its management, in such circumstances wider effects would probably be more readily contained. Thus it proved possible to wind down the positions of the companies in the Drexel Burnham Lambert Group in a relatively orderly way after the collapse of its holding company in February 1990. Nevertheless it might be sanguine to push this distinction too hard, since such a failure might not always be seen by the markets as an isolated one, and might itself trigger actual and perceived difficulties for counterparties. It might also be over-sanguine to assume that only the

failure of a major institution could make the crisis a systemically serious one. In a market crisis where confidence was already extremely fragile, the initial failure of a smaller firm or a regional firm might create the conditions for further price falls which would bring down larger firms. When all this is said, however, it is the major international houses whose failure in a widespread collapse in securities markets would necessarily pose the greatest systemic threat, because of the scale of their operations and their interconnections (either as parts of banking groups or as counterparties of banks) with the banking system.

44. Consideration of the stages by which systemic risks can escalate from securities price fall to securities markets crisis, from market crisis to a crisis for securities intermediaries, and from them to a banking and financial crisis leads logically to a similar separation of the policy and operational issues which arise at each stage and at the transition from one stage to the next.

45. As has been already pointed out, the origin of the first stage is largely taken as exogenous in this report. This does not imply, however, that no consideration needs to be given to the anticipation of problems which increase the likelihood of a sharp fall in securities prices.

46. At the broadest level of macroeconomic policy, monetary policies steadily directed towards price stability themselves make financial crises less likely: conversely an inflationary environment increases financial fragility. More specifically supervisors and market practitioners each need to take note of and provide against such potential precursors of financial disturbance as rising indebtedness, low risk premia, concentrations of risk, and fierce competition in new markets and instruments. Temporary or sustained exposures to leveraged buyouts by investment or commercial banks might be possible examples of this in the current environment.

47. The transition from the first to the second stage raises questions of market organisation, market capacity, interconnections between securities and derivative markets, the use of new trading techniques, and settlement and clearing systems. Malfunctions in these arrangements may aggravate the difficulties caused by a fall in prices. Order handling, order execution, price formulation, clearing and settlement can all be viewed as rings of the same chain: if one of them breaks orders are not received, or executed, or settled. Moreover non-integrated systems are dangerous. If one phase works at a higher speed than the following phase then a bottleneck develops which, in disturbed conditions, can generate paralysis or panic. Settlement problems are especially critical in this respect because they suspend the flow of payments and reduce market liquidity at a time when it is most needed. These issues are considered at greater length in Sections E and F below.

48. The third stage, a crisis for market intermediaries, raises problems of the risk management of the major players in securities markets, whether banks or non-bank securities houses, and of the supervisory régimes applied to them. Issues which arise in terms of supervisory coverage and capital requirements are discussed in Sections G and H below.

49. The final stage of a full-blown banking crisis is less a matter for analysis in this report than the outcome which structural and regulatory improvements shown to be desirable by its analysis would be designed to avoid. Some comments are nevertheless made in Section G on the possible implications for the provision of official safety nets.

E. Market mechanisms

Market structures

50. There are essentially two sorts of models of securities markets -- "dealer markets" and "auction markets". In both types of market, re-pricing and transaction opportunities can evolve continuously. Dealer markets seek to enhance liquidity by providing continuous two-way pricing, with a group of market makers standing ready to quote prices in acceptable market parcels and acting as principals in transactions. Auction markets emphasise an efficient discovery process for stable prices by requiring all orders to interact. Trading is mainly done through brokers who accept instructions to buy or sell securities on behalf of customers. Price trends in broker markets are therefore determined by customer orders, rather than primarily by market intermediaries.

51. The distinction between dealer and auction markets can be drawn too sharply, and is becoming increasingly blurred, as different markets incorporate features of both approaches. The arrangements on the New York Stock Exchange, for example, combine elements of both dealer and auction markets, with dealers handling large deals on their own books "upstairs", i.e. off the floor, and then crossing them on the floor of the exchange. Specialists matching orders for particular stocks on the floor also accept the added responsibility of maintaining fair and orderly market conditions by dealing from their own books as necessary. Existing evidence on the relative efficiency of dealer, auction and combined dealer/auction markets is mixed, so that it is impossible to conclude empirically that one market structure is superior to another.

52. Trading arrangements in individual securities markets and stock exchanges reflect a mix of factors; among them, the character of the saving process in an economy is important. Countries in which savings tend to be mobilised by large institutions, as in the United Kingdom for example, tend to have dealer markets. Institutional investors at times need to trade large parcels of securities, which require the high degree of market liquidity associated with dealer markets (or the combination of dealer and auction markets found in United States specialist systems). In countries where savers tend to participate more directly in managing their assets, usually with small investors having a relatively prominent role, as in Germany for example, auction markets, with their emphasis on price discovery and stability, tend to dominate. In some countries, e.g. the United States, both sorts of markets are available.

53. The two types of markets differ in their need for capital. The capital endowment of intermediaries in dealer markets tends to exceed that for intermediaries in auction markets since, in the former, market makers take risks onto their books while, in the latter, investors trade off their own capital. This distinction is, however, to some extent immaterial for the largest securities houses active in international markets since, even if their domestic equity market is an auction market, they will need capital to back the positions which they take in other markets such as international bond markets.

54. Since market makers deal with large institutional investors, they often take positions which are large in relation to their capital base. This type of market therefore also tends to produce greater concentration of risk than pure auction markets. From this perspective, it is possible to argue that systemic risks are greater in dealer than in pure auction markets. This, of course, is not a case for replacing dealer markets with auction markets but is a case for focusing attention on the risk-management practices of market makers.

55. Strains showed in both dealer and auction markets in the crash of October 1987. Experience varied from market to market but liquidity proved to a degree illusory in both types of markets because, although a large volume of orders was handled, some orders were unsatisfied. Systems which had normally provided timely and accurate information to market participants failed to do so consistently. As

quotation systems became overloaded in dealer markets and quotes were delayed, market makers widened bid-ask spreads, reduced the value of acceptable market parcels and resisted opening up new positions. On some exchanges, "fast markets" were declared, so that dealers were not required to stand behind quotes. All of these measures helped business to continue at, by normal standards, a relatively high turnover. But they reflected the difficulties in meeting the actual demands at the time.

56. Problems were also evident in auction markets. Extreme price volatility subjected all market participants, but particularly small investors, to additional losses as the speed of order execution slowed in response to the emergence of bottlenecks at each stage of the trading process: order placement, routing, matching, execution and information dissemination. Market liquidity declined sharply as many buyers of securities remained on the sideline waiting for prices to steady before coming into the market. This partly reflected confusing price signals and partly the expectation that bargains would be more attractive later.

57. It is difficult to conclude from the available evidence that one approach performed markedly better than another during the market breaks of 1987 and 1989; or, although intermediaries carry greater risks in dealer markets, that any firm preference should be accorded on systemic grounds to one kind of market structure over another.

58. Questions about the optimal structure of securities markets organised in exchanges leave aside the fact that many securities transactions, especially in bonds, are conducted outside exchanges. The French authorities in particular see this as a cause for concern on systemic as well as on other grounds (such as its effect in reducing market transparency and in making insider dealing and other forms of market manipulation harder to detect). While it would certainly be easier for regulatory authorities to monitor securities transactions if they were all conducted on recognised exchanges, it is unlikely that there would be a sufficient international consensus of countries willing to pay the possible price in terms of reduced competition and higher transactions costs for granting organised exchanges the effective monopoly required to bring this about. Moreover even if all the leading national securities (or just equity) markets were exclusively organised in exchanges, and those exchanges were prepared to supply information to each other, major international intermediaries would still be conducting other transactions, e.g. in foreign exchange and money markets, outside exchanges. The supervisory problem (considered in Section G) would thus remain of how to cover the total financial operations of such intermediaries. This is not to deny that transparency is itself helpful to investors, intermediaries and regulators in identifying risks as well as for other reasons; it is a desirable feature of trading arrangements to be set alongside other desirable features such as liquidity and cost. Regulators can, of course, impose trade and price reporting requirements which they consider necessary on off-exchange deals, as is done, for example, in the United States and the United Kingdom.

Capacity

59. Securities market capacity is of systemic, as well as technical, concern. When the flow of reliable market information is disrupted, the quality of investment decisions suffers. If capacity constraints are unforeseen, investors may suffer from liquidity illusion and underestimate their risks when markets are overloaded. This was evident in the United States in October 1987 when many large institutions assumed huge equity positions, in part through the optimism engendered by a long bull market, but also in part based on the perception of substantial liquidity in the stock, options and stock index futures markets which evaporated when they placed abnormal demands on those markets. These institutions, and the market as a whole, did not take into account the stress on liquidity that could be caused by a number of money managers and large institutions simultaneously executing similar trading decisions and strategies. Since the conditions in which overloading occurs are likely to combine high turnover with high price volatility, the resulting delays between order and execution impose price risks on investors and on position-taking intermediaries.

60. Intense use of market systems produced severe operational malfunctions on many stock exchanges during the crash of October 1987. When prices fell sharply in October 1989, however, systems on major exchanges seemed generally to cope better. Improved performance partly reflected measures adopted after the earlier experience. Additional computer capacity on Wall Street coped with the high volume of trading, and co-operative arrangements between regulators seemed adequate. In London the number of trades was lower than in 1987, but the total number of system transactions and "peak loads" were higher. A "fast market" was called at one point when prices were rebounding after Wall Street's recovery but, overall, the International Stock Exchange's systems handled the volumes comfortably.

61. Other factors in the better performance in the later episode were that United States institutional investors were more cautious in their trading and hedging strategies; and in the United Kingdom (in sharp contrast to 1987) market makers had broadly balanced opening books.

62. Further development in the automation of securities markets may in some respects be helpful in improving systemic protection (although the possibility of computer breakdown introduces a new form of systemic risk). So far this process has been carried to various stages in different stock exchanges with the main progress coming in price quotation and order routing. No major securities exchange has yet, however, fully automated its trading mechanism. This partly reflects fears by exchange members that their own role will be reduced. It is also unclear that investment institutions would willingly give up the power which they have in dealer markets to negotiate the best price. It is claimed by market makers that automated execution systems for other than small customer orders increase the scope for other market participants to pick them off by reacting to news before they have time to adjust their quotes. They contend that this would decrease their willingness to make markets and provide liquidity. Whether or not that would be the case, there remains a more general systemic doubt whether any automated dealer system would be as capable as present unautomated market maker systems in dealing with lumpy order flows from large institutional investors, especially in a crisis.

63. This said, automated trading arrangements would have some obvious advantages; they add to market visibility, improve the accuracy and timeliness of information, add to order handling capacity, and tend to integrate the market. They can be used to provide timely information to regulators as well as market participants and thus improve the ability of both to identify and control risks. These benefits may, however, flow more certainly from automating settlement as distinct from trading processes. For example, proposed electronic arrangements for settling bonds in Australia will provide on-line information to traders and their banks about relevant exposures.

64. In short, the October 1987 market break highlighted the need for market systems adequate to process efficiently a high volume of trades. Improved trading systems are clearly desirable and some exchanges have augmented significantly their trading capacity. Yet beyond a certain point, new capacity, installed to deal with relatively rare peak loads, can be costly -- particularly when there are potentially more pressing claims on an exchange's resources, e.g., for improved settlements systems. Moreover, in extreme periods, any system may become overloaded; better systems capacity alone may not be able to meet sharply increased demand for liquidity. In the final analysis sellers do not have an automatic right (especially in auction markets) to expect buyers to be waiting to purchase their stock.

65. In this vein, analysis of market mechanisms following the 1987 crash, while acknowledging the need for adequate system capacity, has tended to focus on measures to contain price volatility and limit trading techniques that might add "artificially" to volumes of trades and volatility. In particular, official working groups and academic studies, especially in the United States, have focused on programme trading in cash and derivative markets; and different forms of circuit breakers. The remainder of this section discusses these issues, and that of the margin requirements for futures trading.

Programme trading

66. Programme trading is defined by the New York Stock Exchange as the simultaneous purchase (or sale) of fifteen or more stocks with a total value of $1 million or more. Several trading strategies are facilitated by programme trading, including index arbitrage, portfolio insurance, asset allocation and index substitution. Two techniques have attracted particular attention: index arbitrage and portfolio insurance.

67. Index arbitrage exploits discrepancies between the price of an index futures contract and the cash prices of the component stocks in the index. Thus, if at a particular time -- allowing for transaction and carrying costs -- the futures price is cheap, arbitrageurs will buy futures and sell the corresponding cash stocks, thereby securing a risk-free return. The effect of such arbitrage is normally to ensure that the two markets concerned move in step. They only do so, however, when the two markets are functioning properly: in the conditions of October 1987 the absence of sufficiently firm prices for many component stocks removed any firm basis for the calculation of comparative prices needed for such arbitrage. In such conditions cash and derivative markets may become unlinked or, under extreme stress, activities in derivative markets may transmit pressures to cash markets.

68. Different authorities have drawn different lessons about index arbitrage from the experience of October 1987. In London, for example, where trading in index futures and options has been on a far smaller scale than in the United States, the International Stock Exchange concluded that the major deficiency of the index futures market was insufficient arbitrage, rather than the reverse (10). A similar conclusion was reached in several other exchanges, where the implication was drawn that steps should be taken to facilitate index arbitrage on grounds that it might enhance market liquidity and, hence, stability.

69. On the other hand, there is a school of thought in the United States which views index arbitrage as an important potential channel, if not source, by which surges of volatility are transmitted from the derivative to the cash markets. On this view the development of index futures and index options has provided a mechanism, which did not previously exist, for large institutions to trade the index rapidly and in large amounts, which can at times impose huge demands on liquidity in the cash market. (That impact is believed by exponents of this view to derive in large part from the high leverage accorded stock index futures through low margins -- an argument considered in paragraph 93 below.) Although this line of argument appears to raise questions about institutional behaviour and about market capacity as much as it does about the technique of index arbitrage, it leads its proponents to favour measures to limit the use of the technique in extreme conditions.

70. Various curbs on programme trading have in fact been introduced in the United States. The New York Stock Exchange (NYSE) has, among other measures and proposals, requested its member brokerage firms to refrain from programme trading unless it would be stabilising, especially on any day when the Dow Jones Industrial Average (DJIA) moved by more than fifty points, and requested that these firms ask their customers to refrain from programme trading. In addition, a formal request by the NYSE for a rule change that requires index arbitrage transactions to be executed in a market stabilising manner when the DJIA declines or advances fifty points was approved by the Securities and Exchange Commission (SEC) in July 1990. The New York Stock Exchange has released the report of a broad-based panel representing leading industrial companies, NYSE member firms, academia and individual and institutional investors. Entitled "Market Volatility and Investor Confidence" (7 June 1990) (11), the report concluded, among other things, that index arbitrage is a natural feature of the linkage between the equity and equity derivative markets and is not, in itself, undesirable; nonetheless the report supported the proposed restrictions by the NYSE to limit index arbitrage in volatile markets because it was felt that such restrictions might have a positive impact on investor confidence. Finally, a bill to give the SEC authority to regulate programme trading is before the United States Congress.

71. It seems fair to draw the following conclusions:

a) Stock index futures serve an important economic function in facilitating the management of price risk through hedging strategies. The achievement of these gains depends importantly on maintaining a tight pricing relationship between futures and stocks, and index arbitrage plays a key role in keeping prices in the two markets in line.

b) There are concerns, however, that during periods of abnormal price movements index arbitrage activity may intensify pressure on stock prices and on market mechanisms by transmitting extreme price movements from the futures markets.

c) Exchanges may deal in part with pressures on market mechanisms by adding extra capacity to accommodate unusual volumes of trading. Some exchanges also have proposed constraints on index arbitrage trading in volatile markets. While such curbs possibly might ease pressures on prices and systems temporarily, they run the risk of further delinking the markets at critical times.

d) The co-ordination of regulation among the markets that trade these tightly linked instruments is important to assess properly and contain the risks associated with various trading strategies. The absence of co-ordination among markets that are separately regulated, but effectively unified through market activity, can increase confusion in abnormal conditions. Co-ordinated regulation may reduce the probability of major market disruptions.

72. The other form of programme trading prominent in 1987 was portfolio insurance. In substance this is a version of the traditional stop-loss order. Instead of selling cash stock when prices fall to a particular level, the portfolio insurer will normally aim to sell index futures, which is quicker and easier. As prices in the cash market fall, the objective is to convert an increasing proportion of a portfolio into hedged (risk-free) form. Thus the portfolio insurer has an upward sloping demand curve; as prices fall he can sell stocks or futures.

73. Portfolio insurance has been adduced as one source of instability in the equity markets in 1987 in two respects. First, it probably helped to prolong the rise in prices on Wall Street during the bull market preceding the crash by allowing investors to believe that they would be protected against a turn in the market. While this could work for an individual investor acting in isolation it could not do so for investors as a whole. Indeed its use arguably weakened the ability of the market to fulfil its proper function of signalling prices. Those who engaged in this form of trading may have been bamboozled by the new technological wrappings with which an old technique was presented. Second, the process of selling into a falling market itself accelerated the fall in prices in both cash and derivative markets.

74. The experience of October 1987 will itself have reminded traders and investors forcibly that the protection provided by portfolio insurance can be illusory. That should itself act to reduce resort to such insurance, at least in the medium-term while memories are fresh. Portfolio insurance has in fact now fallen into virtual desuetude as a result of investor experience. In the longer run, however, investors will always be attracted by techniques that promise to allow them to get out first. Since, however, such techniques can take alternative forms it is questionable whether it makes much sense to seek to ban any particular technique. Thus, for example, the SEC's report on October 1989 (12) found that dynamic hedging strategies akin to portfolio insurance continued to be used, but they were employed by broker-dealers to hedge options written for institutional investors rather than by the institutional investors themselves as was the case in 1987.

75. More generally, sentiment against programme trading hardened further in some sections of the community in the United States after the experience of mid-October 1989. In consequence, some market participants responded by curbing programme trading. The responses both of the New York Stock Exchange and market participants reflect, to an important extent, efforts to restore confidence in the stock market as a place to do business and encourage more favourable public perceptions about it. This is understandable even although it remains open to question whether the effect of programme trading has been as great as these responses imply.

Circuit breakers

76. Circuit breakers can be defined as the imposition of a restriction or an interruption to trading designed to moderate market disturbances; they can be classified into three main types; those related to the volume of trading; those related to price movements; and those which are left to the discretion of market authorities. The basic rationale for all of them is that calling a halt to disorderly trading will allow time for emotions to cool, information to be disseminated and digested, and the balance of supply and demand to be assessed more accurately.

77. The argument for volume-based circuit breakers is that when the volume of trading passes a certain point market systems such as price display and telephone capacity can no longer keep up. In such circumstances, a genuine market often no longer exists. It may be better to impose a temporary closedown in the hope that the storm will blow over. In practice, market authorities have to make judgements about the degree of market malfunctioning. An alternative to closing down the market completely is suspension of certain normal rules. An example of this is provided by the "fast market" arrangements on the International Stock Exchange, under which the normal obligations of market makers to quote firm prices can temporarily be suspended. Users of the market can continue to deal but know that they do so at their own risk. United States exchange and over-the-counter markets employ similar fast market procedures in addition to price-based circuit breakers. A limited version of a discretionary circuit breaker is also frequently found in auction markets, e.g. the German stock exchange authorities may in special cases decide to delay or temporarily suspend the official price fixing of a particular security.

78. The case for price-based circuit breakers as stated by the United States Working Group on Financial Markets (13) is that it is desirable to "substitute planned for unplanned, ad hoc trading halts without increasing the overall frequency of such disruptions". This group observed that extraordinary price movements trigger ad hoc and destabilising market closings. The Working Group also recognised the need for reopening procedures "designed to limit the duration of the halt while providing for information dissemination to permit consideration of buy or sell decisions during periods of stress". Another argument for such circuit breakers is that "free" price movements will very often be exaggerated in terms of the eventual change in prices. According to this argument, circuit breakers may help to prevent such overshooting by giving market participants a short time to assess their positions and avoid decisions based on uncertainty, lack of information, or even panic. In its recent report on "Market Volatility and Investor Confidence" already referred to above, the special task force appointed by the New York Stock Exchange cited such arguments as the basis for their recommendations of a four-tier circuit breaker to be co-ordinated across all United States equity and equity derivative markets.

79. The case against price-based circuit breakers rests on the view that they intrude arbitrarily into the price formation process, since it is impossible to specify in advance at what point markets become disorderly. The most efficient form of adjustment in economic terms to a new equilibrium may well be a step change in prices and, if this were achieved, it would arguably be preferable, for a number of reasons, to a prolonged slide in the market. Thus circuit breakers can interfere with price discovery and prevent markets from clearing. One complication is that, when circuit breakers are in force, traders cannot close positions they might prefer (or be required) to liquidate, even at a loss. If there are no corresponding limits

in other financial markets, pressure may be diverted to them once circuit breakers become operative elsewhere. It is conceivable, for example, that -- if the demand for liquidity were large and could not be met by sales of equities because circuit breakers were in place -- this demand might be met by sales in bond or other asset markets; this might transmit systemic concerns elsewhere in the financial system or real economy. Moreover, even a co-ordinated shutdown of a single national financial system might not prevent the diversion of selling pressure to other countries and could accelerate the transmission of shocks across borders.

80. Even if co-ordination at the national level succeeds in calming market volatility, it cannot deal by itself with the problem of co-ordination with markets in other countries which are open when a market halt occurs or reopen before trading restarts in the suspended market. This may not be a conclusive objection when the closed market is the dominant trading market but it could become a more acute issue, particularly for smaller countries with open financial markets, if and as 24-hour global trading develops on a larger scale. Moreover, it would be difficult to establish circuit breakers for genuinely international markets, like the euro markets.

81. Arguments for co-ordination of trading halts, at national or international level, also beg the question whether in some circumstances it might actually be desirable, for price discovery purposes or to enable investors to transact, to keep associated markets open. It would seem perverse, for instance, to close a market which was coping with an exceptional order flow simply because a less efficient associated or competing market could not cope. More generally, transfer of risk among investors is a crucial function of securities markets. If they were not available, or open only when circumstances were favourable, investors might be less prepared to accept long-term risk, with adverse implications for capital formation.

82. The success of trading halts depends on their having the intended calming effect on sentiment. Unless action is taken while a market is closed to establish a new equilibrium price at which it can reopen with some hope of stability, the market may simply lurch from one trading halt to another. But establishing equilibrium prices for each stock traded on an exchange would present its own problems.

83. Preplanned circuit breakers can permit the preparation of contingency plans well ahead of a market closure and eliminate uncertainty associated with discretionary market halts. But a familiar problem with rules announced in advance is that markets may adapt their behaviour to take account of them and, so far as possible, to circumvent them. Thus, for example, in circumstances where the market is falling towards a "limit-down" price, investors may be encouraged to unload their positions in case the circuit breaker is triggered and the market re-opens at a yet lower price. It is this kind of consideration, together with a reluctance on principle to close markets except in extremity, which lead many market authorities to prefer to retain discretion whether and when to halt trading.

84. Empirical evidence on this topic is both limited and mixed. Bertero and Mayer, in the study referred to above, found that prices on national markets which had circuit breakers of one form or another had somewhat lower price falls in the days following the 1987 crash than others. Cantor (1989) (14) finds that, for soybean meal futures markets, the United States market (with price limits) tends to have more large price changes than the United Kingdom market (which does not have price limits). The Commodity Futures Tading Commission (CFTC), in consultation with Federal Reserve staff, have examined daily price movements for contracts in which limit moves had occurred with enough frequency to allow meaningful analysis. This examination provides no evidence of magnet effects, which would result if anticipatory trades accelerated the movement of prices as they approached prevailing limits.

85. Circuit breakers came into play in the United States during the episode of mid-October 1989. On the Chicago Mercantile Exchange (CME), the S&P 500 futures contract hit an initial price limit at twelve points down, which lasted almost thirty minutes, and a subsequent price limit at thirty points down,

which would normally have lasted for an hour but because it was triggered in the last hour of trading remained in effect till the close of business. The hitting of the initial price limit at twelve points down brought into effect the New York Stock Exchange's "side-car" procedures whereby automated programme trades are put in a separate file for five minutes. Orders are then executed unless the change from the previous price exceeds a certain limit in which case trading in that stock would be halted. Trading was halted in the S&P 100 options index on the Chicago Board Options Exchange shortly after the first CME price limit was hit and trading did not re-open that day.

86. The effect of these circuit breakers has been examined in great detail by United States regulatory agencies. In its final report, Trading Analysis of 13 and 16 October 1989 (May 1990) referred to in paragraph 74 above, the SEC staff found that the circuit breakers which were triggered may have relieved the pressure from the diversion of orders from the futures to the stock market which would otherwise have resulted from the continuation of index arbitrage sell programmes. Specifically, the report concluded that, among other things, the twelve point price limit for the Standard and Poor's 500 futures contract on the Chicago Mercantile Exchange coincided with a sharp drop-off in the level of programme selling on the New York Stock Exchange and a reduction in the rate of decline in NYSE stocks. After the price limit expired, the rate of the price decline in NYSE stocks increased substantially. The SEC staff concluded that, while a direct causal relationship is difficult to establish, their findings did not indicate any harm to the markets attributable to the imposition of the circuit breaker mechanisms. They also concluded that, given current market and regulatory structures, there can be no assurance that the extraordinary volatility of 13 October and 16 October 1989 will not be repeated or surpassed in the future.

87. Somewhat different conclusions were reached by the staff of the Commodity Futures Trading Commission, in their Report on Stock Index Futures and Cash Market Activity during October 1989 (May 1990) (15). This study concluded that the twelve point price limits did not appear to moderate intra-day market volatility, particularly on 13 October 1989. Instead, the CFTC staff believes there is some evidence that a binding circuit breaker in one market is associated with increased volatility in other unconstrained markets. In addition, they found that the expansion of the twelve point shock absorbers, i.e., when the twelve point limit was replaced by a thirty point limit on the S&P 500 futures market on 13 October 1989, was associated with a significant increase in the overall volatility of the underlying S&P 500 index. Finally, according to the CFTC staff study, S&P 500 index futures were significantly more volatile, and volume was heavier, during this period than the period just prior to the twelve point shock absorber.

88. Although there are divergences of views on the merits of circuit breakers among the members of our group as elsewhere, we broadly agree on the following four propositions. First, circuit breakers of one form or another only come into play when a disorderly market has already arisen. Second, they can in some circumstances be helpful in moderating that disorder. Third, the procedures for reopening as well as closing markets have to be carefully considered. But, fourth, especially in an era of expanding international trading, it would be wrong to presume that their availability could guarantee the containment of systemic contagion in a major market crisis.

Margin requirements

89. Margin requirements are a regular feature of derivative markets throughout the world as well as the stock markets in the United States, Canada and Japan. Except in those countries, they are rarely imposed as a regulatory requirement in stock markets although banks may impose them on customers borrowing to purchase securities. In futures and options markets they are used for prudential purposes to protect dealers against default by customers, and to protect clearing houses against default by their members. In securities markets they also serve to protect lenders. Some believe that they can be used to reduce speculative borrowing to finance securities transactions, although this is not universally accepted.

These differing objectives raise the two main questions about the role of margins in systemic risk analysis; namely their prudential effect, and their effect in preventing speculators from taking highly leveraged positions which might contribute to price volatility.

90. Futures clearing houses impose initial margin requirements on their clearing members when they take out new contracts, and thereafter pay or receive variation margins in line with daily price moves. In addition, United States clearing houses allow the initial deposits made by customers with clearing members to be drawn down without needing to be replenished till they fall below a separate, lower maintenance margin requirement. The initial margin payments are intended to cover one day's price swing and typically might be set on the basis of a 95 per cent or greater probability of success judged by volatility over a given previous period. The question of what the right level is, however, cannot be entirely settled by formula for the obvious reasons that the answer will vary according to the past period taken, that the past is not always an accurate predictor of the future, that the degree of protection that it is reasonable to provide through margin requirements has to take into account other risk management safeguards in the overall régime, and that it would be costly to cover every eventuality. In short there is room for an additional element of judgment.

91. There are some grounds for questioning whether futures clearing houses do always maintain adequate margin levels for the purposes of systemic protection. On 13 October 1989 United States futures clearing houses made calls for additional intra-day variation margin payments. In addition, initial and maintenance margin requirements were raised on both 13 and 16 October. While lower margins may provide adequate coverage of risk for most trading days, raising requirements in a market crisis may impose additional strains on liquidity at the least helpful time. They also reveal a potential conflict of interest between the clearing house, with a natural concern for its own financial integrity, and the pursuit of a wider objective of market stability. This example also suggests that the original requirements in this particular case (though not necessarily in others) were simply too low. For whatever reason they do not appear to have taken into sufficient account the possibility of extreme price movements.

92. If, as the authors of this report consider probable, we have moved into an era where large daily price changes are more frequent but this has not yet been fully captured in statistical analysis, there appears to be a good case for national regulatory authorities to monitor more closely the initial and maintenance margin requirements set by clearing houses and, in cases where they judge it necessary, to encourage them to impose higher requirements. Especially where they are linked to particular exchanges, clearing houses may give too much weight in their own judgment to competitive considerations.

93. Arguments about the effect of futures markets on price volatility tend to mirror those on index arbitrage. Those, including the SEC, who believe that futures markets act as catalysts for price changes in equity markets see index arbitrage as the mechanism by which the investment market for stocks can be whipsawed by the volatile trading markets for stock index futures. They point to the considerable incentives, especially for institutional investors, to substitute trades in futures markets for corresponding trades in stock markets because settlement, acquisition and margin costs combined are lower than those for stocks. Thus traders can control a much greater investment in equities indirectly through futures contracts than through a direct investment in stock, and higher leverage from relatively low margin requirements can add to the volume of speculative transactions in futures markets. Indeed some argue that this gearing ability provides futures traders with the means of exerting enormous selling power in the stock market which could pose a substantial threat to market stability in extreme conditions. Others question whether this does not merely amount to an admission that futures markets are more efficient than stock markets, and argue that it does not follow that higher speculative activity in the former causes higher volatility in the latter, or that too low futures margins lead to such an effect. Buying the market through index futures may, for instance, be a logical and efficient strategy for those fund managers who believe

that they can no longer achieve the informational advantage necessary to pick individual stocks successfully.

94. To some extent this difference of view may, as with index arbitrage, reflect the difference between the experience of the United States with its huge derivative markets and that of European countries such as the United Kingdom and France whose derivative markets are less well developed and smaller not only in absolute terms but also relative to their domestic stock markets. The Deguen Report in 1988 (16) concluded, for instance, that futures markets were helpful in improving price determination. Nevertheless, differences of view on this subject are also marked within the United States both in official and in academic circles. As instances, some studies such as that of Shiller (1988) (17) offer evidence consistent with the view that futures traders tend to overreact to "noise" thereby raising volatility, but others (for example, a Federal Reserve Board Staff Study by Paul Kupiec, January 1990) (18) find no evidence to support the hypothesis that low futures margins increase volatility in the cash market.

95. Regardless of these differences of view, there is a case to be considered for setting initial (and maintenance) margins on financial futures at levels which strengthen the degree of protection for clearing houses and the market against those occasions when large price swings occur.

F. Settlement and payment issues

Introduction

96. In recent years increasing attention and concern has focused on the process of settling deals in securities. This has reflected a number of factors, notably rapid growth in the volume of securities trading (as illustrated in Table 1 below), technological advances, a growing perception of and sensitivity to the risks involved and some particular episodes which have highlighted deficiencies in existing arrangements. In many cases the problems and the response have been viewed largely in a domestic context. But it has also been recognised that the functioning of settlement arrangements has a substantial and growing international dimension, paralleling the expansion of international capital flows.

Table 1. **Some indicators of securities trading volumes ($ bn)**

	New York	Tokyo	London	Euro-bonds
1978	210	160	40	240
1983	780	230	90	910
1988	1 370	2 230	480	4 630

97. Partly in association with the increase in activity in securities markets, there has also been a significant expansion of trading in derivative instruments of various kinds. This expansion came earliest and has been carried furthest in the United States; but in the last few years growth has also been extremely rapid, albeit from a much lower base, in Europe, Japan and several off-shore centres. Settlement arrangements for trades in derivative products are of particular interest and concern from several points of view: first, given the nature of the instruments involved, the management of risk is especially important; second, arrangements for derivatives -- specifically futures -- can in certain respects be a useful paradigm for settlement arrangements generally, given that most so-called "cash securities" markets in fact settle as very short (say one day, three day or five day) futures markets; and third, given the intimate relationship between derivatives and the underlying securities, there are clear advantages in establishing links between

the corresponding settlement arrangements, for example so as to avoid liquidity pressures arising from different settlement timetables and in terms of risk management.

98. The two main objectives in recent reviews of settlement systems have been: to increase efficiency and lower costs, mainly by exploiting technological advances (especially by substituting book-entry transfer systems for systems based on the movement of paper); and to identify, and then either reduce or manage more efficiently, the risks inherent in the settlement process.

Previous studies

99. The intensified interest in settlement questions has stimulated a number of recent studies with a variety of emphases. A summary of the recommendations in the four main reports discussed below is shown in Table 2. In addition, in the context of the current review by the Ad Hoc Group of Experts on Securities Markets, the OECD commissioned a further study by Dr. J.R. Kessler specifically of settlement practices in markets for derivative instruments. His results are reported in his paper "Risks in the Clearing and Settlement System of Markets for Financial Futures and Options" (19), which is expected to be published shortly.

100. Settlement questions figured prominently in the reports produced by United States government agencies and the task forces set up in the aftermath of the October 1987 crash. Amongst the points which these reports particularly emphasised were the need for closer co-operation between, or integration of, settlement systems (Brady) (20), the need for clarification of the legal relationships between clearing organisations and settlement banks (CFTC) (21), the need to increase capacity [the United States Working Group on Financial Markets (22), SEC (23), CFTC (24)], and the need to consider enhancements to risk management arrangements, in the light of the continued growth of trading volumes and the apparent increase in price volatility (the United States Working Group on Financial Markets) (25).

101. A further group of recommendations relating to settlement arrangements was advanced by the ISSA (International Society of Securities Administrators) following their symposium in May 1988 (26). These recommendations addressed a number of general issues (e.g. centralisation of depository and settlement functions), measures designed specifically to reduce risk (e.g. introduction of delivery versus payment and the shortening of settlement periods) and features of settlement systems particularly relevant to cross-border transactions. Participants in the symposium (referred to as ISSA 4) also gave consideration to settlement arrangements in individual countries.

102. Securities settlement has also been of interest to the European Community in the context of plans to achieve an integrated European market by 1992. In 1987 the European Commission asked Dr. J.R. Kessler, formerly of the Frankfurter Kassenverein and the Deutsche Auslandskassenverein, to undertake a study of settlement practices within the Community and to make recommendations for their improvement and linkage. Dr. Kessler completed his report in July 1988 but, because of various technical delays, it did not become widely available until the spring of 1989 (27), somewhat after many of the other studies mentioned here were completed.

103. Another study was commissioned by the Group of Thirty, a group of distinguished international financial officials, academics and practitioners, following a symposium in London in March 1988. The exercise was guided by a steering committee and carried out by a working party who were asked to consider necessary, or at least desirable, features of national settlement systems, as a first step towards improving the efficiency and security of international securities settlement. The result was the promulgation in March 1989 of a report (28) making nine recommendations relating partly to settlement timetables, partly to risk management and partly to system mechanics. Since publication of the report

Table 2. **Summary of ISSA, Kessler, G30 and FIBV recommendations**

	ISSA (May 1988)	KESSLER (July 1988)	G30 (March 1989)	FIBV (June 1989)
<u>Settlement Timetable</u>	-- as short as possible, not more than T+5 for settlement	-- no particular timetable proposed -- should be standardised across Europe -- generally supports G30	-- T+1 trade confirmation (inc. resolution) for market-side -- T+3 settlement, or T+5 interim	-- supports ISSA, Kessler, G30
<u>System features</u>	-- rolling, continuously netted clearing -- dematerialisation where possible in a Central Securities Depository and clearing organisation controlled by users (one per country) -- minimisation of risks e.g. by DVP and careful participant criteria	-- rolling settlement -- one Central Securities Depository in each country -- immobilisation and book-entry transfer -- registered securities via central nominee to ensure good delivery -- CSD should be independent, supervised, financially sound, non-profit making with participant criteria	-- rolling settlement -- trade comparison for investors -- Central Securities Depository with broadest participation and coverage of securities -- immobilisation or dematerialisation and book-entry transfer -- consider trade netting -- registered securities via central nominee -- lending encouraged to ensure prompt settlement	-- each country has a Central Securities Depository -- immobilisation or dematerialisation and book-entry transfer
<u>Payment features</u>	-- DVP: simultaneous final payment (no details)	-- strong emphasis on simultaneous DVP -- links with payment system but CSD processes payments through members (CSD) cash accounts	-- simultaneous DVP -- preferably same-day payments -- payments system may be separate from CSD -- consistent payments arrangements between markets	-- DVP linked to book-entry transfer in CSD for domestic trades -- describes three models for cross-border settlement with and without DVP
<u>International features</u>	-- each country's central organisation to link, with reciprocity and harmonisation of facilities -- international dealings should be settled in home country -- adoption of international communication standards	-- concentration on harmonisation within EC -- standard bilateral co-operative agreements between CSDs -- immobilisation in a lead (usually home) country -- CSDs hold cash accounts with each other to achieve DVP across borders -- adoption of international communications standards	-- concentrates on improving domestic systems as pre-requisite for cross-border developments -- adoption of international communications standards	-- links between each country's CSD -- immobilisation (or dematerialisation) of securities in home country -- adoption of international communications standards -- automated book-keeping and communications systems

continuing efforts have been made to monitor and encourage implementation of the proposals in individual countries.

104. Finally, the FIBV (the Fédération Internationale des Bourses de Valeurs) which had been one of the earliest to launch a review of settlement procedures following a seminar in April 1987, published its conclusions in June 1989 (29). The task force which undertook the review had terms of reference which focused specifically on cross-border settlement issues. Its four main recommendations were: the adoption of the international settlement conventions laid down by three parallel study groups (G30, ISSA and the study for the EC by Dr. Kessler); the setting up or expansion of links between national securities depositories; the immobilisation of securities in the issuer's home country, even in the case of securities owned by an overseas resident; and the stipulation by any exchange listing or trading foreign securities that book entry transfer in the home country's depository (or in an international depository) constitutes good delivery. As part of its work, the task force developed three models for links between national depositories ranging from a simple arrangement for the transfer of title to securities to a more complicated system involving investor sub-accounts in overseas depositories and arrangements to handle payments.

Risks in settlement: individual systems

105. In the context of this paper, the key aspects of the settlement process are the ways in which risk arises and the ways in which it can be reduced or managed. This section (paragraphs 105-124) examines the position in relation to individual settlement systems taken in isolation. Some of the issues relating specifically to the settlement of trades in derivative instruments (futures and options) are set out in more detail in the report by Dr. Kessler, referred to in paragraph 99 above. The next section (paragraphs 125-129) discusses briefly the additional issues which arise in a world where there are many different systems, in different countries and/or dealing with different instruments.

106. Two main types of risk are involved in the settlement process often referred to as "capital risk" and "market risk". Capital risk is the risk that one or other counterparty fails during the process of exchanging securities for money, so that the other counterparty delivers security without receiving money, or vice versa. Market risk is the possibility of a deal having to be replaced at a different price because one or other counterparty fails before the exchange of securities for money takes place. These risks may remain with the original counterparties to a deal, or be transferred in whole or in part to third parties -- very often the providers of payment and settlement services.

107. Capital risk in settlement can be avoided only if the transfer of securities is accompanied by a transfer of money in the opposite direction and both transfers are simultaneously irrevocable and unconditional for all the parties involved. Many of the most important issues in the design of settlement systems arise in the attempt to get as close as possible to this ideal of "Delivery versus Payment" (DVP). In general terms, the possible means of achieving DVP are:

a) **Intra-day finality**, based on real-time money and securities transfer; or

b) **End-of-day finality**, based either (i) on real-time securities transfer and end-of-day money transfer, or vice versa, or (ii) on simultaneous end-of-day securities and money transfer. In the case of (i) any provisional intra-day transfers may have to be unwound. Alternatively, it would be possible for third parties of undoubted credit standing to take on "daylight exposures" on behalf of the original counterparties by committing themselves irrevocably at the time of, say, the intra-day securities transfer to make a corresponding payment in the end-of-day cash clearing. (This looks like DVP from the point of view of the original counterparties, but actually transfers risk to the third parties, typically banks.)

c) **Deferred finality**, whereby transfers are final at some specified or unspecified future time.

108. For such systems to work satisfactorily, it is essential that title to securities and money can be definitively transferred within the framework of the system. In other words there must be a means of ensuring "good delivery" of securities and "good payment" of money, so that there is no question of title proving defective, and a transfer therefore invalid, once it has taken place. The methods used to settle transactions vary widely, in part reflecting different views on what constitutes "good delivery/payment" or, more accurately, "good enough delivery/payment" in the particular circumstances of the market concerned.

109. In the absence of DVP, there are nevertheless a number of ways to reduce, redistribute or protect against capital risk, and also against market risk. Amongst them are:

a) Monitoring of **system membership**;
b) The **shortening of settlement periods**;
c) The use of **netting** arrangements;
d) The introduction of a **central counterparty**;
e) The use of **collateral** and **margin**;
f) **Loss-sharing arrangements**; and
g) **Support from outside** the market.

These are now considered briefly in turn.

110. The **membership** of a settlement system has obvious implications for the risks faced by participants. Most systems lay down requirements of one sort or another for direct membership, which may include financial requirements. Direct members -- sometimes called "clearing members" -- may also clear trades on behalf of non-members. In so doing, they can play an important role in risk spreading and risk monitoring by guaranteeing the performance of the indirect members and thereby forming a buffer between the central clearing house and the rest of the market. Both risk and efficiency considerations will often point to a tiered system, with some of the first tier of direct members being specialist institutions providing clearing, nominee and custodial services to an outer tier of indirect members.

111. The risks of settlement failure are likely to be lower, as is the market risk arising from it, the **shorter is the settlement period** (i.e. the time between dealing and the exchange of securities for money). The two types of settlement arrangements commonly used -- account settlement and rolling settlement -- have somewhat different features in this respect. The former involves the deals during a fixed period being settled on a single day. This enables sales and purchases throughout the period to be netted for settlement, with the potential benefits discussed below (paragraphs 112-115). But it can at the same time lead to an accumulation of settlement obligations, and hence of counterparty exposures, and place considerable strains on systems on and immediately prior to settlement day. By contrast, rolling settlement involves settling a day's deals a set number of days later, so that every day is a settlement day but only for one day's deals. Compared with an account system, rolling settlement breaks up the settlement load and, in the long run, may help to smooth out settlement peaks and troughs. Moreover, if the settlement lag in a rolling settlement arrangement is shorter than the average settlement period in an account system, counterparty exposures have less time to accumulate.

112. **Netting arrangements**, if properly constructed, can make a considerable contribution both to enhancing operational efficiency and to reducing and reallocating risk. The Group of Experts on Payment Systems of the central banks of the Group of Ten countries analysed these issues in the Report on Netting Schemes published in February 1989 (30) and identified a number of potential benefits. This work has been continued and extended in a series of working parties, with a view to putting a further report to

central bank governors later this year. First, netting schemes reduce the number of deals that have to be settled individually and can thereby relieve operational strains. Second, they are likely to reduce the value of the transfers that have to be made, and can thereby help, for example, to reduce liquidity requirements and alleviate the risk of delay (or even gridlock) where banks are employing "caps" (i.e. limits designed to contain daylight credit exposures, to their customers or to each other). Third, by reducing or removing timing differences between inflows and outflows, they may reduce settlement risk and liquidity strains, and thus the risk of failure. Finally, netting tends to reduce counterparty exposures and, consequently, counterparty risk. A practical example of netting arrangements which illustrates some of the potential advantages, but also some of the difficulties, is that of "master" agreements in the swap market. These, besides dealing with the general legal framework for a series of swap deals, typically also include provision for netting.

113. Whether a particular netting scheme secures any or all of these benefits depends very much on the legal environment. Three possible variants are:

a) **Accounting or position netting**, which nets the amounts due to be delivered but leaves the original contracts intact;

b) **Netting by novation** (or obligation netting), which extinguishes the original contracts and replaces them with new (net) contracts; or

c) **Close-out**, under which, if certain specified events (such as liquidation) occur, all outstanding contracts are brought forward for settlement as a single netted amount.

114. **Accounting netting** reduces the volume and value of flows, and thus can help to ease operational strains and day-to-day liquidity requirements, but does nothing to reduce counterparty risk. Netting by **novation** secures the operational benefits of accounting netting but also reduces counterparty exposures. An agreement to **close-out** unsettled contracts in the event of a liquidation (or some other trigger event) does not in itself affect daily settlement flows or the obligations of the parties involved. It should, however, help to reduce counterparty losses in the event of a failure and could thus reduce the risks attaching to a going concern's counterparty exposures.

115. Another crucial aspect of netting arrangements is the number of participants involved. It is usual to distinguish **bilateral netting** between two parties from **multilateral netting** involving a larger group. The latter could entail parties finding that in the netting process they had acquired exposures to other parties with whom they had not undertaken any deal. In many cases this would not be regarded as acceptable, and for this reason many multilateral netting arrangements incorporate a central counterparty.

116. A **central counterparty** can, however, contribute to the security of settlement whether or not it is involved in a multilateral netting arrangement. By taking on an "universal counterparty" role as a principal, it effectively provides a guarantee to participants in a settlement system, in the sense that if a participant defaults either on delivery of securities or money the central counterparty must nevertheless discharge its obligations in respect of the other half of the deal. (In most respects, the risks incurred in acting as a central counterparty are the same as those involved in providing a formal guarantee. The position of a guarantor may be less clear than that of a central counterparty, however, because the original parties to a trade retain direct legal obligations and rights in respect of each other.) A clearing house may guarantee some trades but not others. For example, it may act as a central counterparty for intra-market ("street side") business but not for member-client ("trade side") business. In that case, it is important to insulate the parties to non-guaranteed trades from the risks associated with the clearing house's role as guarantor. This is effectively the position in New York, where the National Securities Clearing

Corporation clears and guarantees intra-market trades and the Depository Trust Company clears, but does not guarantee, broker-client bargains.

117. A system involving a central counterparty can provide a number of benefits. Apart from facilitating multilateral netting of obligations, it enables risk-management and counterparty assessment to be centralised. The chief advantage claimed for such systems, however, is that the central body acts as a shock absorber so that counterparty risk for market participants is significantly reduced. There are, however, several factors on the other side of the balance. First, while a central counterparty arrangement reduces risk for participants in the system it lays the central counterparty (the clearing house) itself open to both market and capital risk (indeed it is exposed twice, once to each counterparty, in respect of any particular deal). A central counterparty will therefore normally seek to protect itself against these risks: it may adopt one of the procedures discussed in paragraphs 125-128 below; and, in relation to capital risk specifically, will have an interest like all other participants in achieving effective DVP.

118. The second disadvantage arises from the concentration of risk and the fact that the resources supporting a central counterparty will normally be limited (i.e. it will not have unrestricted access to the central bank). (This was illustrated by the rescue which had to be mounted in October 1987 for the Hong Kong Futures Guarantee Corporation, the body which guaranteed trades on the Hong Kong Futures Exchange.) Those resources must include the liquidity necessary to make payments on the due settlement date, irrespective of whether participants in the system have themselves made payment to the centre. If a central counterparty suffers a loss which it cannot absorb, and in consequence is unable to meet its own settlement obligations, the effects would clearly be serious and pervasive (q.v. the example noted above). They may indeed be so serious and pervasive that the relevant financial authorities have little option but to intervene. It follows that the central counterparty must keep its risk exposure under continuous review and take appropriate action to contain and protect against that exposure. It must in addition have clear procedures in the event of a member's default, clear rules about what obligations it will accept or reject and adequate resources to meet the ones it accepts.

119. Third, a risk pooling arrangement, like that introduced with a central guarantee or counterparty, is likely to involve some degree of moral hazard for the participants. They may be inclined to adopt less rigorous standards themselves in assessing the credit quality of their counterparties, in the knowledge that any failure will be made good by the centre and that they will bear only a (small) proportion of the overall cost.

120. It is possible to protect against and/or reallocate the risks arising from credit exposures, both in a central counterparty system and in one which preserves the original bilateral contracts. Two techniques are the pledging of collateral and the calling of margins.

121. A **collateralised** system works on the basis that any extension of credit -- whether by a trader, a bank, a clearing house or some other party -- is secured on readily realisable, high quality assets. This has the effect of redistributing some of the risk from the lender to the unsecured creditors of the borrower. In a book entry transfer system, collateral can conveniently be provided if participants are able to grant a legal security interest over assets which they hold in the system and, in particular, over those assets which they acquire through the system and in relation to which they are seeking credit. The attractiveness of these assets as collateral to a lender will obviously depend on their liquidity; it is, in addition, crucial that the legal security is enforceable speedily and without exposure to challenge in the event of a member's insolvency. This is a particular problem, at least under the national law of some countries, in the case of securities held or acquired on an "agency" basis (i.e. on behalf of a customer acting as principal).

122. The pledging of **margin** when a trade is executed (or matched or entered into the settlement system) can help to protect against market risk. (Since margin arrangements are usually operated in the

context of a system with a central counterparty, the protection is usually being given to the central counterparty.) The protection can thereafter be maintained by regular marking-to-market and the calling of variation margin. In some countries, the national law reinforces this position by giving clearing organisations a preferred status in the event of a member's insolvency, so that they are able to deploy margin (or enforce other security pledged by members) without hindrance from normal insolvency procedures. The precise balance of risk and cost to the various parties is affected by whether margins are levied on a gross or a net basis. Most markets use net margining but some, including the Chicago Mercantile Exchange, margin gross. The choice is significant, as it can have a very large effect on the way the financial burden is distributed between hedged and unhedged participants in a particular market. Furthermore, margining itself is exposed to settlement risks insofar as both initial and variation margins themselves have to pass through a clearing system. It is essential, for example, that the counterparties (and where appropriate their banks) should know precisely when margin has unconditionally changed hands.

123. Another approach which a central counterparty might employ in protecting itself against the risks it has taken on, or that the participants in a settlement system may themselves use directly to protect against these risks, is some form of **loss-sharing agreement,** based either on: (i) subscriptions to a members' fund; or (ii) an obligation on members to make contributions -- or further contributions -- in the event of a loss. Such a system would be subject to the moral hazard problem mentioned in paragraph 119, especially if subscriptions were collected from all members whether or not they had traded with the defaulting member. Allocating risks to the original counterparties of a defaulting member might, however, have arbitrary results in markets where each member was obliged to trade with all other members or where the dealing system did not readily permit a choice of counterparty -- e.g. in open outcry markets or automatic execution systems.

124. A further option to cover settlement risks is **external support**, which might for example take the form of a guarantee or a letter of credit provided by a banking syndicate, or of insurance. Either of these would redistribute risks away from the system's members and in so doing might help to transfer losses occasioned by a major default to a part of the financial system which was otherwise immune and which was able to bear the loss without risk of insolvency or knock-on effects (i.e. it might be desirable from the point of view of handling systemic risk). There would correspondingly, however, be moral hazard unless the providers of the guarantee or insurance were able to differentiate very accurately the prudential behaviour of different members of the system.

Risks in settlement: systemic issues

125. Settlement arrangements are important from the point of view of systemic risk for two reasons: first, they are a source of risk in their own right; and second, and more important, they can play a crucial role in transmitting the effects of a member's failure to other members, and thence to the financial sector more widely. It may be helpful first to clarify in just what sense settlement systems are a source rather than a transmitter of risk.

126. For the most part, risks in settlement arise not from inadequacies in the internal workings of settlement systems themselves but from the potential insolvency of members of these systems. There have, however, been cases where an internal system failure has caused serious disruption to the extent that the solvency of members could have been put at risk (such an episode occurred in November 1985, when, as a result of a computer breakdown, the Bank of New York had to borrow $24 billion overnight from the Federal Reserve Bank of New York). A second potential source of such internal risk is the way in which different settlement systems interact. If systems are incompatible, in the sense that they involve, for example, different timetables for collecting and paying out cash, they are likely to impose increasing strains on users as turnover rises, as may happen at times of market disruption. These strains, which may begin in terms of liquidity, can easily be translated into problems of solvency. It is worth noting in passing that

dispersion of settlement arrangements can have other disadvantages; it can inhibit or limit the use of netting as a means of risk reduction and make more difficult the process of risk monitoring both for the operators of settlement systems and for the regulatory authorities.

127. Almost as a matter of definition, settlement is the channel through which counterparty risk is crystallised and transmitted. The effect may be direct, exposing other members of a settlement system to the financial losses (or gains) associated with market risk and capital risk. It may, less frequently, be indirect -- through the failure of a central counterparty -- where that failure has itself been brought about by the default of a system member. The transmission may clearly take place whatever the arrangements for settlement; the risks are intrinsic to the process of settlement itself. What organised settlement systems do is not (generally) to introduce new risks but to offer the opportunity to reduce or redistribute the intrinsic risks in a way which provides better protection for participants in the markets and the system as a whole.

128. Settlement across international boundaries does not raise fundamentally new issues of principle. All or most of the points mentioned earlier in this section are relevant in an international as well as a domestic context. What the international dimension does is greatly to increase the practical difficulties of achieving some of the risk reduction or transfer mechanisms described. Some examples are as follows. First, cross-border systems are likely to have to operate within a mixed legal and fiscal environment which complicates the business of ensuring definitive transfer of title to securities, enforceable netting arrangements and so on. Second, final transfer may in any case only be possible in the home country of the security or currency involved. Thus legal title to registered stock will often only be transferable in the books of the issuer's own registrar, and final transfer of money only in the books of the issuing central bank. Third, time delays, whether because of time differences or communication difficulties, are likely to be greater and it may be hard to adhere to the same timetable for both domestically and internationally originating transactions. Cross-border settlements also involve issues of foreign exchange risk, exchange controls and, in certain instances, restrictions on information flows (e.g. arising from banking secrecy provisions in one of the states involved).

129. The approach recommended by the G30 and others to such problems could be characterised as convergence, i.e. each country should seek to enhance its own domestic settlement arrangements in line with some agreed principles, with the hope or expectation that the degree of convergence will in due course allow links between systems to be established relatively easily. An alternative, represented by Euroclear and Cedel, is the centralised system, based in a particular jurisdiction but with access open to all those who can meet the membership criteria. This approach may help to overcome some but not all of the difficulties mentioned in paragraph 128.

Conclusion

130. Settlement arrangements are a key element in the transmission of financial disturbances, and as such can potentially play a major part in the reduction and management of systemic risk. The way they work in practice is, however, very much conditioned not only by their mechanical operating procedures but also by the legal environment. Since these environments differ significantly from country to country, there is a limit to the applicability of general prescriptions. There are, however, a number of objectives, identified in recent reports and in this paper, which if achieved would expose and then help to contain the risks involved in settlement.

G. Supervisory coverage

Diversity of present arrangements

131. A survey of the countries represented on the ad hoc group -- which thus included most countries with major securities markets -- confirmed that there are large variations between different national régimes for the financial supervision of securities business. There are considerable differences in institutional and functional coverage, in the legal status of supervisory authorities, and in the number of authorities within different countries. Partly in consequence of these differences there are also large variations in the financial requirements imposed by different authorities, which are discussed in Section H.

132. These variations in supervisory coverage reflect differences in market structure, in stages of development and in the activities which different kinds of institutions are permitted to perform. In this last respect a principal source of variation springs from the extent to which banks can participate in securities markets. In the universal banking countries, such as Germany and Switzerland, securities business (e.g. proprietary trading, new issue underwriting, secondary market making, and agency transactions on behalf of customers) is generally regarded as banking business. At the other end of the spectrum, such as in Japan and the United States, banking and securities businesses are legally separated (although this separation is beginning to break down at the edges in both countries and is under official review in Japan). In these countries, the types of securities activities in which banks may engage are restricted. In the United States, for example, banks are generally limited to acting as principal and agent for government and certain public debt securities and to acting as agent for customer transactions in corporate securities. However, where other securities activities cannot be carried on by a bank, they may be permitted in a foreign or domestic affiliate. In other countries, such as Belgium, Canada, Finland, France, Greece, Italy, Luxembourg, the Netherlands, Portugal, Spain, Sweden, and the United Kingdom, a third, hybrid type of regulatory structure exists where both banks and non-banks participate in the securities markets.

133. Given this variation in permitted activities it is hardly surprising that national supervisory régimes vary greatly in their coverage of banks and non banks conducting securities business. In Austria, Belgium, Canada, Denmark, Finland, France, Germany, Greece, Ireland, Luxembourg, the Netherlands, New Zealand, Portugal, Spain, Switzerland, and the United States, securities activities carried out by banks on their own balance sheets are regulated by the appropriate banking supervisor. Capital adequacy requirements are applied to the banks' activities as a whole and do not at present appear explicitly to account for all securities-related risks (although this is envisaged for all EC countries from 1993 onwards). With the exception of Canada, Spain and the United States, it appears that securities firms owned by banks in these countries, where they exist, are also regulated by the domestic banking supervisor and that supervision is carried out on a consolidated basis. In Canada, banks' in-house activities are regulated by the banking supervisor whereas banks' securities affiliates are regulated by provincial securities regulators and self-regulatory associations. In the United States, the SEC regulates all securities firms including those that are bank owned. In the United Kingdom banking and securities supervisors have overlapping responsibility for securities business undertaken by banks on their own balance sheets. When it is conducted through bank-owned subsidiaries these fall under the jurisdiction of the securities regulator, and have to meet its capital requirements: the Bank of England, as banking supervisor, does not consolidate the accounts of such a subsidiary into that of the banking group as a whole but nevertheless oversees the management of the whole group. Subordinated loans to the subsidiary are deducted from the bank's capital.

134. Supervisory coverage of securities firms which are not affiliated to banks also varies between countries. For instance, in Austria, Ireland, and the Netherlands, stock exchanges provide the primary regulatory vehicle. In Australia, Belgium, Canada, Greece, Italy, New Zealand, Spain and the United States, broker/dealers are regulated by the equivalent of securities commissions. (In Italy there are

currently proposals before the legislature to replace the present regulatory arrangements by a comprehensive régime to be operated jointly by the Bank of Italy and the Consob, under which the Bank of Italy would conduct financial supervision of all kinds of firms engaged in securities business while the Consob would be responsible for ensuring that they complied with other regulatory requirements for e.g. disclosure and conduct of business. A similar division of responsibilities is also planned in Portugal.) In Switzerland all financial institutions acting as primary dealers are regulated by the Banking Commission. In Austria, Denmark, Finland and Sweden all securities firms are regulated by the banking supervisor (as they will also be in Luxembourg in future), although in Denmark banks and non-banks are subject to different rules. Supervision of securities firms outside the banking system in these countries is carried out on an unconsolidated basis. In the United Kingdom, all investment businesses are regulated either by functional self-regulating organisations (SROs) recognised by the Securities and Investments Board (SIB) or directly by the SIB. In Japan the Securities Bureau of the Ministry of Finance is the supervisory authority. In some other countries securities firms outside the banking system do not yet appear to be subject to any capital adequacy requirements.

135. There are also differences in supervisory coverage of securities, futures, and options markets and market participants. In most major financial markets, a single regulator has ultimate responsibility for regulation of securities, futures and options, although the day-to-day oversight may be divided among various government and self-regulatory organisations. In the United States, on the other hand, the Securities and Exchange Commission (SEC) regulates stocks and stock options, while the Commodity Futures Trading Commission (CFTC) regulates stock index futures (as well as other financial and commodity futures). There is considerable discussion within the United States concerning this division of responsibilities and its implications for co-ordinating inter-market mechanisms like clearance and settlement systems, margin requirements, circuit breakers, enforcement and global regulatory issues. The United States Administration has proposed legislation transferring the authority to regulate stock index futures from the CFTC to the SEC, the intent of which is to unify regulation and to enhance co-ordination of key intermarket mechanisms.

136. To what extent is this diversity in national regulatory coverage a cause for international systemic concern? It might be such a cause for concern if:

a) Inadequate standards in some countries led to a competition in laxity to attract business; or

b) Significant risk-taking activities by major intermediaries were left unsupervised; or

c) Diffusion of responsibility for the supervision of conglomerates either

   i) Among different functional supervisors and/or
   ii) Among different national supervisors

   failed to deliver a sufficiently comprehensive oversight of the risk exposure of such conglomerates; or

d) Differences in the status, coverage and objectives of the national supervisory authorities impeded international co-operation among them.

Supervisory standards

137. With the internationalisation of securities markets and the activities of the largest intermediaries operating in them there must always be some temptation for the latter to move or book some of their

operations to centres with no or low financial or other regulatory requirements. At the same time, however, there are likely to be strong countervailing pressures to do business in well regulated centres; and those centres may in any case provide more favourable locations for business in terms of political and economic stability, infrastructure, expertise, etc. Greater convergence in standards would reinforce those pressures. For this reason the various current international initiatives to make progress in this direction -- through the International Organisation of Securities Commissions (IOSCO), Basle and the EC -- are to be welcomed. The technical issues which arise are discussed in Section H.

138. The justification for such convergence would lie partly in a need to maintain adequate prudential standards across world markets, and partly in assuring reasonably even competitive conditions for intermediaries of varying national ownership. The standards likely to emerge from international negotiations which have both these underlying motives are likely to reflect something of a compromise between them. Up to a point, this need not be a bad thing. The levels at which capital requirements are set is inevitably a matter of judgment in any case. Requirements could be set so high that failure of a major intermediary conforming with them would become virtually impossible; but by the same token that would discourage the degree of innovation and risk-taking which is desirable for healthy market development. Nevertheless, there is a case, discussed further in Section H, for incorporating a safety margin in capital requirements to give greater allowance for extreme price movements.

Standards of risk management by intermediaries

139. There could even be some danger in over-reliance on detailed capital requirements if their existence led managements and supervisors of financial intermediaries to assume that they need do little more than observe and monitor compliance with the rules. What is also critical, given an appropriate set of rules, is the quality of the risk-management of the intermediary. Conversely, effective supervision does not rely excessively on the observance of mechanical formulae but encourages the managers of intermediaries to improve the quality of their risk-management, and thus reaffirms the principle of management responsibility.

140. Surveys by the international accountancy firm Klynveld Peat Marwick Goerdeler (KPMG) conducted in 1988 and 1989, based on interviews with senior executives of over one hundred leading international banks and securities houses, suggest that a good deal of progress has been made over the past two years in increasing awareness of the need for, and in improving the quality of, in-house risk management. They also suggest, however, that there was plenty of room for improvement. Both the experience of the October 1987 crash, and the new rules brought in by banking supervisors under the Basle agreement of 1988 and by some securities supervisors (especially in the United Kingdom and Japan) have acted as spurs.

141. Several other findings in KPMG's "Global Report 1989" (31) bear on the issues considered in this report. The use of mathematical models in trading options and other new instruments has advanced, although a few houses still do not use them, and questions remain whether all senior managers fully understand the risks taken by their traders. Greater attention is, however, being given to sensitivity analysis of the effects which a given change in, say, interest rates will have across the whole of a group's book. This kind of approach -- which KPMG term risk consolidation -- seems to be a more effective use of management time than an attempt to monitor in detail all the transactions reported to the centre by all the operating parts of the group. KPMG report, however, that as yet few houses have fully comprehensive consolidated systems bringing together the sensitivity of the group's operations to a variety of trading risks. This tends to confirm how important it is for supervisors to assess the quality of the risk control systems which managers of financial intermediaries operate.

Gaps in supervisory coverage

142. A prior condition for such an approach to supervision, however, is that significant risk exposures of the intermediary come within the coverage of a supervisor in the first place. In this respect, the absence in some countries -- of which the United States has been by far the most important -- of regulatory accountability for affiliates, subsidiaries and holding companies of regulated (non-bank) securities dealers potentially adds to systemic risk. This enables regulated firms to move many potentially risky activities that fall outside the scope of the securities regulators, such as interest rate swaps, bridge loans, and foreign currency transactions, out of the regulated firm to unregulated entities within the same group. Since these activities would attract significant capital charges if conducted in the regulated firm, and since large losses on them could potentially cause as much damage as losses on regulated activities, they ought in principle to be subject to supervision or at least to reporting requirements and supervisory oversight. It makes it difficult for the securities regulator to evaluate the operations and financial stability of regulated firms without a thorough understanding of the overall corporate structure to which they belong.

143. For this reason the SEC has put forward to the United States Congress legislative proposals to enable them to obtain financial information concerning the affiliates, subsidiaries and holding companies of registered broker-dealers. The enactment and implementation of this legislation would begin to plug the single most significant gap in the current regulatory coverage of internationally important securities intermediaries. Experience of the Drexel collapse, which vividly illustrated the spread of contagion from non-regulated to regulated entities within a group, has now given greatly added momentum to the progress of these proposals in Congress. Their proposals would not provide the SEC with regulatory authority for currently non-regulated activities. Nevertheless the power to obtain information would put them in a position to assess the potential exposure of the regulated firms from the unregulated entities, which could result in their taking special steps to ensure the financial integrity of the registered broker/dealer. With the right degree of co-operation between supervisors and managements, the proposed new reporting requirements could provide the springboard for regular assessment of the total risk exposure of the broker/dealer to related entities.

144. The problems caused for supervisors by diversion of operations to non-regulated entities within a group become more complex when these are located outside the jurisdiction of the home country supervisor. In an ideal world they would be greatly reduced, though not wholly removed, if regulators in all countries where securities operations were permitted exercised a comprehensive supervisory coverage over risks taken by securities firms incorporated within their jurisdiction. This ideal may ultimately be achievable in OECD countries and in major non-OECD financial centres, but it is unlikely that regulation havens could be entirely eliminated from the map.

Supervision of international groups

145. Even if there were no gaps in national coverage of specific activities, and no variations in the standards of supervision applied by different nations, there would still be problems for the individual national supervisors in forming an overall assessment of the financial strength of a group engaged in international securities business; and thus the extent to which it was a source of strength or weakness to the component entities under their own supervision. While this should not be a serious disadvantage if they all perform their own functions effectively, a diffusion of responsibility among separate national supervisors may in practice leave open the possibility that inadequate attention will be paid to intra-group exposures and to the impact of a failure of one part of a group on the others. In concentrating upon their own particular responsibilities, separate national supervisors may fail to give sufficient priority to such potential risks of contagion -- and, hence, to the systemic risks with which this report is concerned.

146. Further layers of complexity are added when account is taken of the existence of separate functional as well as national supervisors responsible for the supervision of different kinds of intermediaries active in international securities markets -- banks, specialist securities dealers, and conglomerates which combine within their group these and other kinds of financial and, in some cases, non-financial business. These arguably make it all the more desirable, though more difficult, to establish a mechanism for co-ordinating the activities of the different supervisors, for arranging proper exchanges of information and for clarifying and strengthening the relationships between them.

147. The first priority in tackling these issues on which all members of the ad hoc group agree is for the appropriate national regulators to obtain and share with each other information regarding regulated and unregulated entities of the major intermediaries active in international securities markets, in order to enable each regulator to assess the potential impact of the activities of the rest of the group on the entity for which it is responsible. There would be every advantage if banking and securities supervisors stepped up current efforts to increase practical international co-operation through bilateral agreements on exchanges of information. Better information on related entities of a firm in other countries would put home and host country supervisors in a better position to respond to international or other major disturbances which might adversely affect the financial condition of the firm or the markets. The personal contacts made, and trust built up, in the process of arranging exchanges of information would, moreover, themselves be valuable when it came to co-ordination of action in a market crisis. The series of memoranda of understanding between the SEC and some of its counterparts in other countries for exchanging information concerning breaches of national securities laws is a useful precedent.

148. The exchange of information does raise several important issues. First, problems of confidentiality need to be resolved, particularly where self-regulatory organisations are involved. Second, the use to which the recipient supervisor can put the information must be defined, and the supervisor supplying the information must be consulted before the recipient takes any remedial action. Third, any legal impediments to exchange of information must be explored and resolved. In some cases such impediments may be overcome with the consent of the regulated entity. Finally, the type of information to be exchanged, and the regularity with which it is exchanged, need to be specified. It is important that material information be exchanged at least on an ad hoc basis, but preferable that there should be a regular exchange of information, supplemented by ad hoc exchanges in circumstances where this would be particularly helpful.

149. The question arises whether more needs to be done than improving exchanges of information to establish a more systematic international mechanism for co-ordination between supervisors. A variety of possible approaches to this issue may be considered. At one end of the spectrum would be a deliberate attempt to contain the risks within the individual parts of a group by the erection and maintenance of "firewalls" between them, putting the onus entirely on the individual supervisors of the separate entities; at the other would be consolidated supervision by one overall group supervisor. In between would be systems where some combination of approaches, involving co-operation between different functional and national supervisors, would be adopted.

150. There was naturally also a spectrum of opinions on this issue within the ad hoc group. The SEC representatives on the group took the firm position, consistent with their own domestic legislative proposals, that expanded reporting requirements and exchanges of information would be sufficient to give individual supervisors the information they needed to make judgments about the impact on their regulated entities of activities elsewhere within the group; that this approach would significantly reduce risk; that there was no need to regulate holding companies directly; and that consequently neither full-blooded consolidated supervision, nor even a more qualitative system of central oversight under the leadership of the principal home country regulator were necessary or appropriate policy objectives at present. Other

members of the group either felt that the latter approaches positively should be the way forward, or retained open minds on the question. So this report discusses some of the options.

151. The first option, that of firewalls, amounts to a rationalisation and reinforcement of the present system of dispersed supervision of international conglomerates. Activities would be conducted in separate subsidiaries subject to separate supervisors according to function and national location. Emphasis would be put on the insulation of the separate parts from the rest of the group. Exchanges of information would, in this scenario, be designed to strengthen the insulation by making it easier for the individual supervisors to identify and control intra-group transfers of capital. Firewalls of this kind would be consistent with the laws of limited liability. They would enable the supervision of separate activities to be conducted by the functional supervisors who had the relevant specialist expertise. Capital could be dedicated to the separate corporate entities to match the risks which they individually undertook. The operations of any non-financial parts of the group could be put at a greater distance from the financial operations. There would be no need to widen access to official safety nets beyond any banking operations within the group. Moral hazard could thus be minimised.

152. All these claimed advantages depend upon the critical assumption that risks can be contained within the separate parts of a group. The question is whether this assumption is ultimately robust. Especially where banking operations are involved, it leaves out of the reckoning the effect on the confidence of depositors and counterparties if any company within the group is allowed to fail. The same questions concerning the effects on the confidence of counterparties would arise if a major non-bank securities firm were put in the same position. This was indeed demonstrated by the Drexel collapse; once the holding company was unable to fund itself, it became impossible for other companies within the group to maintain funding and retain normal dealing relationships with their counterparties. The only option open was to wind down all their operations in as orderly a manner with the least disruption to markets as possible.

153. Full consolidated accounting supervision by one recognised main supervisor would evidently be the most comprehensive solution to this issue of overall supervision of a financial conglomerate. In an interim report prepared for discussion with other banking supervisors and with securities regulators, the Group of Ten banking supervisors have recently recognised the arguments in favour of this approach in relation to the consolidation of banking and securities business. They have put forward the view that, since positions in the same instrument taken by different entities within a financial group are normally interchangeable, then the market risk positions of all those banking and financial entities in a group whose business involves taking such risks (i.e. in currencies, interest rates and equity positions) need to be measured on a consolidated basis. This would remove any scope for counting the same capital base more than once as a cushion against risks, and would prevent risks taken in unsupervised locations from escaping measurement -- though care would need to be taken that netting of offsetting positions across separate companies did not result in understating total risks. There would be practical difficulties, however, in adopting a fully consolidated approach in some countries and to some forms of financial conglomerate. In countries where separate supervisory régimes are applied to banking and securities business (and in the absence of agreement on identical capital requirements for market risks undertaken by banks and non-bank securities houses, as discussed in Section H) there would be the political as well as technical problems entailed in altering existing regulatory structures. In those countries, concerns might be raised that consolidated supervision of a group would replace expert by possibly less expert supervision, would lump together disparate balance sheets to which different forms of prudential requirements applied, could mix financial and non-financial business together, and could be taken to imply an enhanced degree of official responsibility and support for the whole diverse array of activities conducted by conglomerates. In the case of groups which contained companies underwriting insurance risks as well as companies taking credit and position risks, for instance, there would be problems to be overcome in consolidating different kinds of risk to which different prudential criteria are applied under existing supervisory régimes.

154. A different approach, which is already applied to some extent in some countries such as the United Kingdom, would be to establish some form of central oversight over financial conglomerates, short of full accounting consolidation but going further than bilateral agreements to exchange information and to co-operate between national and functional supervisors with separate jurisdiction over companies within a group. Especially in the case of predominantly banking or predominantly securities groups that would correspond more closely with the way such groups are actually managed than does separate supervision of their component parts. Such central oversight would not necessarily require full accounting consolidation or, still less, the application of uniform risk measurement techniques where these would be inappropriate, e.g. in assessing the financial position of a group including separate banking, securities and insurance companies. It would rather be a matter of employing both quantitative and qualitative information to produce a central assessment of the risks to which the group was exposed. This approach would also allow some judgement to be made on the extent to which non-financial operations within the group were a source of strength or weakness to the banking, securities or other financial operations without going so far as to assert direct supervisory jurisdiction over or responsibility for them. Indeed, any attempt at direct supervision of non-financial activities of a conglomerate looks impracticable.

155. How might such a system of central oversight of the operations of the major intermediaries active in international securities markets be developed? At the international level the Basle Concordat between banking supervisors has established understandings on the allocation of responsibilities between home and host country supervisors which give primary responsibility for solvency to the former. The EC is taking the same approach both for banks and for securities firms through its proposals for a second banking co-ordination directive and an investment services directive. If non-bank securities supervisors outside the EC concluded that assigning a primary responsibility for the supervision of groups was desirable, they could consider whether and how to follow these precedents, and seek to establish their own wider international consensus. To meet the concerns expressed here such a consensus would need to cover the supervisory treatment of subsidiaries and affiliates of the main company as well as its branches.

156. The machinery for establishing international understandings between securities supervisors is not as well established as that between banking supervisors. IOSCO has been making appreciable progress in the last few years in creating a forum for international discussion between securities regulators but has not yet proved itself as a vehicle for securing international commitment to common action. This partly reflects the diverse composition of its membership which follows from the diversity of national supervisory régimes described at the beginning of this section. Nevertheless sufficient recent progress has been made to encourage hopes that IOSCO can play an effective role in co-ordinating action by its members. It is highly desirable that it should.

157. The pursuit of separate paths to international co-ordination by banking and by securities supervisors is itself less than ideal in this connection, though this again reflects institutional realities. If a system of central oversight of the kind discussed here were to be developed it would require understandings to be reached on the allocation of responsibilities between different functional supervisors as well as different national supervisors with similar functional responsibilities. These might have as their outcome either the recognition of the primacy of a single home-country institutional supervisor where this was feasible (as would be most readily the case with groups such as universal banks where one activity and one supervisor predominated) or alternatively some system of shared responsibility between several supervisors with one acting as primus inter pares. The lead regulator arrangements for the supervision of financial conglomerates in the United Kingdom provide one model for the latter kind of arrangement. Another possible model might be constructed on the basis of a distinction between financial supervision of a group, to be exercised by a single institutional supervisor, and regulation of the conduct of separate entities within the group, to be exercised by the appropriate functional regulators in different countries. Other approaches or combinations of different approaches (in recognition of the existing variety of supervisory régimes in different countries) might also be explored.

Some implications for official support

158. It may be objected that any attempt to centralise and integrate the financial supervision of the major financial groups operating in international markets would increase expectations of official support in times of crisis and so encourage rather than discourage reckless behaviour. This anxiety is the stronger against the background of various bank rescues in the last decade and, most ominously of all, because of the development of widespread insolvency within the United States "thrift" industry and the consequent huge costs which accrued to the United States Government in meeting the obligations of the Federal Savings and Loans Insurance Corporation. In this context arguments for expanding the circle of institutions to which explicit or implicit obligations of official support should be given do not fall on receptive ears in finance ministries and central banks. Nor do they accord with the traditional approach of specialist securities regulators with their emphasis on providing protection to investors through disclosure and transparency of information, and through investor compensation schemes, but not through support of failing intermediaries.

159. In discussion of these arguments several distinctions need to be made. First, provision of general liquidity -- the most usual form of central banking support in a market crisis -- differs from direct support of individual institutions. Second, the provision of liquidity in a securities market crisis goes more directly to the principal securities dealers in countries where these are banks or subsidiaries of banks than it does in countries where it needs to be channelled through the banking system to independent securities dealers, and where its arrival at the right destinations consequently also depends on commercial judgments. Third, in those rare cases where governments or central banks might judge it expedient to organise or themselves directly carry out rescues of banks or other financial institutions, the existing shareholders would customarily still lose their money (or they would participate in the rescue and be required to inject new money) and the existing management would be replaced. Neither shareholders nor senior management can therefore draw much personal comfort from any expectation of official support in a crisis, which suggests that moral hazard may be exaggerated as an influence on their behaviour. Nevertheless the existence of safety nets may be expected to have some effect in dulling the necessary sense of critical vigilance in managers, customers and creditors of protected institutions.

160. There is also some confusion as to whether the purpose of depositor protection and, to a lesser extent, investor compensation schemes is to buttress the system by removing any incentive to make withdrawals of funds or whether it is simply to assure a limited degree of protection to small depositors and investors. If they provide full or very generous compensation to depositors or investors in the event of the failure of a bank or other financial institution, then this may indeed shore up confidence in the system but at the expense of reducing the need for depositors or investors to discriminate between prudently and imprudently managed (and even between honest and fraudulent) intermediaries. The moral here is surely that it is better to set protection of small depositors and investors as the prime objective of such schemes by limiting compensation payments to a modest maximum. (There is also a case for limiting compensation to a proportion of the loss incurred as an incentive to discriminate between intermediaries but some members of the group were not persuaded of the desirability of anything less than full compensation up to a ceiling, especially for investor compensation schemes.) Such limited schemes still make a positive contribution to systemic assurance, on a more modest and manageable scale.

161. In any event, if some integrated international system of central supervisory oversight could be developed its purpose would be to reduce, not increase, the risk that official intervention might be required. It would probably be best to confine any such scheme, at least initially, to those large international players whose failure would most obviously threaten systemic damage. No explicit or even implicit guarantees of support applying to any failure in any circumstance of an intermediary within the scheme would be attached to it. The conclusions of the current review by the United States Treasury in its deposit insurance study of the issue of institutions "too big to fail" may well be relevant in this context. Indeed the principal

authorities involved in such a scheme should consider at the outset the benefits of continuing to operate what President Corrigan of the Federal Reserve Bank of New York (32) has termed a policy of "constructive ambiguity" about their responses to any future contingency.

H. Capital requirements

162. The equity market crash in October 1987 underlined the fact that one of the most important tasks facing regulators and securities participants is ensuring the financial integrity and responsibility of the worldwide securities market place. In the past decade, the risks assumed by firms engaged in the securities markets have increased dramatically. Today, firms risk a substantial amount of their capital in complex trading strategies involving securities, futures, currencies, and interest rate swap vehicles in the world's securities markets. The failure of a large player in the securities markets could seriously affect other major firms, clearing systems, and lenders as well as the overall functioning of the financial system. To provide adequate protection against such an occurrence, a capital adequacy rule should be designed to encompass the risks faced by a firm. Some of these risks include adverse price movements of securities or financial instruments held by a firm and the failure of a counterparty. An appropriately designed capital standard should ensure that if a firm suffers losses, it continues to operate in a financially sound manner. It should protect counterparties, customers, and creditors by reducing the possibility that financial problems at a firm will cause it to default on its obligations.

163. Although there are a wide variety of firms in the securities markets worldwide, in terms of regulation there are two principal categories: (1) banks, whose securities activities generally are only one part of their total activities and generally have been a minor part of those activities (although in some countries securities activities are a major part of some banks' business); and (2) non-bank securities firms, whose predominant activities are acting as agents or principals in securities or derivative products such as futures and options.

Capital standards for banks

164. Bank supervision of capital adequacy proceeds from a much different basis than does supervision of securities firms. Traditionally, banks have invested most of their funds in illiquid assets such as secured and unsecured loans to customers funded by highly liquid deposits and borrowings and by capital. Banks traditionally have held these assets to maturity, and therefore, the credit risk is the most important risk that bank regulators must address. These assets are not marked to market and generally are accounted for on a cost basis.

165. In the recent past, however, banks in some countries have begun to syndicate loans and to aggregate consumer loans, securitise them, and sell them in the market place. Thus, there has been a tendency for banks in some countries to hold their loans for shorter periods of time. In addition, in some countries, securities activities are becoming an increasing part of the business of banks.

166. With respect to securities activities of banks, many countries distinguish between investment account assets and trading account assets. Generally, in these countries, investment account assets are accounted for on a cost basis and trading account assets are valued at market prices or the lower of cost or market price. Where different valuation rules are used, defining which securities fall into which category becomes important.

167. Even with banks involved in securities activities, bank supervisors have tended to focus on one of the traditional risks in the banking business, credit risk, rather than market risk, which is one of the

basic risks intrinsic to non-bank securities firms' activities. Because market risks typically have been small relative to banks' overall net worths, bank capital rules have not focused on this risk.

168. The Basle Committee on Banking Supervision formed under the auspices of the Bank for International Settlements located in Basle, Switzerland, issued a paper (33) ("Basle Accord") containing proposals for risk based capital standards for international banks. These standards will be phased in by 1992. The focus of the Basle Accord principally is on broad categories of credit risk and a uniform definition of capital. The Basle Accord recognised, however, that other risks, notably interest rate risk and investment risk on securities, need to be taken into account by supervisors in assessing overall capital adequacy. As discussed subsequently, the Basle Committee has established various sub groups to examine possible approaches to address these risks.

169. In general, under the Basle Accord, a bank will be required to maintain, at a minimum, total capital equal to 8 per cent of its risk-weighted assets. Under the Basle approach, capital is defined as assets minus liabilities but includes certain subordinated debt and reserves. In general, capital includes shareholders' equity (common stock and preferred stock), retained earnings, certain subordinated liabilities, and certain kinds of reserves. For purposes of the Basle Accord, capital is divided into two classes. Tier I, or Core Capital, includes common stock holders' equity, perpetual preferred stock, and retained earnings. In computing Tier I capital, the bank must deduct any carrying value for goodwill. Tier II, or Supplementary Capital, includes redeemable preferred stock, liabilities initially subordinated to creditors for a period of over five years, and certain reserves against assets. Under the Basle Accord, no more than 50 per cent of the bank's qualifying capital may be Tier II capital.

170. Risk-weighting is the process of assigning prescribed weights to classes of assets and potential assets (e.g., draw-downs on letters of credit issued by a bank). Generally, the weights are based on preconceived notions of credit risk as to each class. The weights vary from 0 per cent for government securities to 100 per cent for obligations of corporate debtors. Hence, for each $1 000 in government securities on its balance sheet, the bank would be required to have $0 capital, but for each $1 000 in loan receivables from a corporation or in corporate securities, the bank would be required to have $80 in capital. In order to cover risks not dealt with in the Basle Accord, bank supervisors may apply additional or higher weightings or set capital standards exceeding 8 per cent if they judge it appropriate in light of the activities undertaken by an individual bank.

171. Banks and their subsidiaries and bank holding companies generally are subject to consolidated regulation and supervision. The principle of consolidated supervision, insofar as capital adequacy is concerned, means that the capital available to support a banking group's activities should be assessed against the total value of the risks being incurred by the group (i.e. similar to treatment of individual banks). Total risks normally are calculated in terms of credit risk. However, in some countries such as the United Kingdom, consolidated supervision for capital adequacy purposes is not required of securities subsidiaries regulated by a securities supervisor.

Capital standards for non-bank securities firms

172. Securities regulators' approach to capital adequacy differs in major respects from the Basle Accord. Securities firms generally take positions as short-term traders and have to be able to meet losses as they occur. This leads to an emphasis on i) marking securities and commodities positions to market to reflect current value, thus including any losses incurred even though no transaction recognising that loss has taken place, and ii) position risk requirements that provide a margin of safety against potential losses that may be incurred as a result of market fluctuations before a position can be liquidated. The capital of securities firms must be adequate to withstand losses associated with specific risks encountered (i.e.

position, settlement, and other basic risks). This has led securities regulators to treat illiquid assets conservatively.

173. Non-bank securities regulators regard credit risk in securities positions as being subsumed by position risk and the mark-to-market requirements; although some supervisory authorities from countries with universal banking systems take the view that credit risks, interest risks and price risks should be separated. If securities were held by a non-bank securities firm in its trading book, a deterioration in the creditworthiness of the issuer of that security generally would be reflected in a falling security market price. The non-bank securities firm would have to reduce its capital by the amount of the market decline as well as the position risk requirements on the reduced market value. The sudden and abrupt failure of an issuer with publicly traded securities without warning occurs infrequently, and, generally, such a risk is small.

174. In systemic terms, the risk which appears most likely to cause the greatest concern is an overall market crash of the kind seen in October 1987. A specific development, affecting a single security, could conceivably cause the collapse of a single firm, although this risk ought to be minimised by appropriate requirements limiting exposures to one issuer. But widespread problems would be more likely to stem from a general market adjustment of an extreme kind, although a price collapse in the securities of a particular widely-held sector (e.g. real estate or a class of securities such as junk bonds) might also cause difficulties for more than one firm.

175. The objective of the requirements for non-bank firms in a number of countries is to reduce the likelihood of firms failing but with the subsidiary aim that, if firms do experience difficulties, it should be possible to close them down without sums owed to clients or counterparties. The need to avoid widespread failures on systemic grounds might be translated into a need for position risk requirements which covered every eventuality, however extreme. This would be to go too far. Securities regulators need to be satisfied that a reasonable but not an excessive allowance is made for the possibility of extreme price movements. Otherwise, requirements which were excessive relative to the overall risks would simply have the effect of stifling activity. With additive requirements this means not covering each extreme eventuality with every one of the requirements. It is unlikely that in the short term a firm would be experiencing the same shock on all parts of the balance sheet (equities, bonds, foreign exchange, counterparty risk). In addition, in certain countries firms have to meet a base requirement which provides an extra cushion, although that cushion should not be viewed as a substitute for appropriate risk haircuts. Moreover, with the daily marking to market firms must adjust their capital to cover past price falls and thus provide a margin of safety against potential losses over the next 24 hours. When all this is recognised, however, the increased possibility of extreme price falls widely spread among international securities markets may still point to the need to incorporate some additional systemic safety margin in position risk requirements.

176. Following changes introduced by Japan at the beginning of this year, capital requirements for non-bank securities firms will be based on a net liquid assets test in all the larger markets. The objective of this test is that a firm should be able to wind down its activities quickly and repay all of its liabilities including the claims of other securities houses and customers. In a net liquid assets test, all illiquid or intangible assets are deducted from capital, and most unsecured receivables are also deducted from capital. After these deductions a firm must have sufficient capital to cover position, counterparty, and settlement risk and to meet a base requirement to cover unmeasurable risk.

177. Securities regulators like the banking supervisors place emphasis on a core of owners' equity. In many countries, they allow the use of subordinated loans to cover part of the capital requirements. The amount of subordinated loans allowed is greater, however, and the term required is shorter than banking supervisors permit. This enables firms to meet their fluctuating risk-based requirements, and if a firm were to encounter difficulties, the funds provided by the subordinated loans would be used to meet obligations

of the firm to customers and counterparties. The use of subordinated loans as capital are, however, generally subject to certain conditions. For example, repayment by the non-bank securities firm to the lender is not permitted if it would result in a firm's capital falling below a threshold set above its required level of capital. Furthermore, the degree to which subordinated loans can be used is limited relative to owner's equity.

Efforts to harmonise capital standards

178. The above discussion illustrates that the capital standards traditionally applied to the banking and securities industries differ. There are differences in the definition of capital, in valuation of assets (e.g. marking assets to market versus the use of cost), and in perceptions and treatments of risk. For example, in many countries, banks generally value investment account securities at cost while non-bank securities firms value all securities at market value.

179. The capital framework of the Basle Accord is a significant advance in achieving greater harmonisation of capital adequacy requirements for banks. While the framework continues to focus on credit risk, the Basle Accord recognised the need also to focus on market risk. As a consequence, the Basle group has established a number of sub groups to study various aspects of risk: one sub group has been considering interest rate risk, another sub group has been considering position risk on traded equities, and a third group has been considering foreign exchange risk. Incorporation by banking regulators of market risk requirements into their rules will better focus those rules on the actual risks encountered by banks in their dealings in foreign exchange, money and securities markets.

180. There has also been some useful progress in preparing the ground for convergence of non-bank capital adequacy standards. The Technical Committee of IOSCO appointed a working group to examine the risks applicable to securities firms. That group produced a report entitled Capital Adequacy Standards for Securities Firms (34). Its conclusions were: i) there is a need for a common worldwide conceptual framework regarding the capital requirements for non-bank securities firms; ii) the capital requirements of the common framework should include risk-based elements covering all the risks to which a firm is exposed; and iii) minimum capital requirements should be based on the type of business being conducted by a firm so that firms wishing to enter the securities business demonstrate a level of commitment to the business, but should not be so high as to affect competition adversely. At its annual meeting in September 1989, IOSCO endorsed the conclusions of that report and asked the Technical Committee to continue its work in this area, to consider how a more detailed common framework can be developed, and to consider ways in which international financial supervisory arrangements can be improved. To the extent that these efforts result in the adoption by securities regulators of comprehensive risk-based capital requirements, risk to the overall worldwide financial system will be reduced.

181. As part of their 1992 internal market programme, the member countries of the European Community have been developing proposals for capital standards for investment firms. Because the main dealers in securities in the community range from the universal banks which dominate securities business in Germany to the London-based subsidiaries or branches of American and Japanese owned non-bank securities houses, the problem of reconciling the two different approaches to capital adequacy described in the preceding paragraphs has arisen in an acute form: at the same time because of the 1992 timetable it has had to be addressed more urgently than in other fora. The Commission of the EC has put forward proposals which tackle this problem by giving banking supervisors in member states the choice between applying the existing 8 per cent solvency ratio directive to all of a bank's activities, including its securities trading operations, or allowing banks to separate out their investment trading books and making them subject to the same provisions on position and counterparty risks as would be applied to non-banks. If the latter option were taken, banks would also be allowed to apply the same definition of capital as non-banks

to their trading book i.e. with a higher proportion of subordinated debt, thus creating a concept of Tier 3 capital for Tier 3 risk.

182. While this formula falls short of the fully integrated approach which Germany in particular would prefer it does enable member countries to take into account questions of the relative competitiveness between banks and non-banks in deciding which option to take, and potentially accommodates the continuation of alternative corporate structures by allowing decisions on whether or not banks should conduct their investment business through separate subsidiaries to be determined by commercial judgments rather than by regulatory requirements. This formula also has the advantage that it does not sharply conflict with or pre-empt the course of the wider international discussions in Basle and IOSCO. It will remain important for the sake of wider international convergence that, as and when further progress is made in those fora in harmonising international capital standards and/or in integrating the tests applied by banking and securities supervisors, the European régime should be flexible enough to accommodate further adaptation as necessary. As matters stand, important differences of view remain to be resolved in all three fora, inter alia on the separation of types of risk referred to in paragraph 173, on the weighting of different assets, on the appropriate allowances for hedging, netting and diversification, and on the competitive disadvantage which non-banks are perceived to incur from the application to them but not to banks of base capital requirements related to e.g. three months' expenditure.

183. In order to reach a better understanding of the differences between the existing requirements in different countries both for banks and non-bank securities firms, each OECD Member country has been sent a notional balance sheet of a non-bank securities firm and a bank involved in some securities activities. Each bank and securities regulator in the OECD member country has been asked to compute the capital of the bank and non-bank securities firm in the example. When they become available, the results of this comparative exercise should be most helpful in increasing the understanding not only of the OECD but also that of the regulators working through IOSCO, Basle and the EC to set common minimum standards.

Conclusions

184. Securities supervisors should continue to explore the desirability of more consistent international capital adequacy standards that would enhance stability, liquidity, and confidence in domestic and international markets. In doing so they should give due weight to the increased possibility of extreme price movements spreading rapidly across securities markets internationally.

185. Bank supervisors should continue their efforts in seeking to incorporate in their capital adequacy standards market risk capital requirements for banks' securities business.

186. Harmonising capital requirements for banks and non-bank securities firms is a formidable task, complicated by differences in the nature of the core business of the two types of institution (on the liabilities as well as the assets side of the balance sheets) and in the established approaches of banking and securities supervisors. Some members of the group believe that this requires identity of treatment in the requirements imposed on both sets of institutions, others that broad equivalence of treatment would be both appropriate and sufficient. Current international efforts need to continue to be pursued intensively to achieve workable solutions.

Summary and conclusions

187. National securities markets are becoming more interdependent. Over the past decade prices of securities traded on them, especially equities, have become more liable to move in the same direction.

188. In particular, some studies suggest that markets have become more prone to extreme concurrent price movements. It would be prudent for securities regulators to work on the assumption that securities markets have become more susceptible to large, precipitous price falls which would be rapidly transmitted around the world.

189. Such price falls would not necessarily but could bring harmful systemic consequences. Defaults by major intermediaries (or clearing houses) could occur, and, if they did, might set in motion defaults by other intermediaries on a scale which could disrupt the banking and payments system generally, which would in turn be likely to harm real saving, investment, and growth.

190. On the other hand the ability of the monetary authorities to act in time to prevent financial crises from developing far enough to wreak such damage has arguably also increased. Official readiness to relax monetary conditions may, however, itself encourage excessive buoyancy in securities markets, and expectations of support for failing firms may encourage imprudent behaviour by intermediaries.

191. These considerations reinforce the case, valid on wider grounds, for maintaining counter-inflationary monetary policies which should help to reduce excessive buoyancy and volatility in securities markets. But they also give the monetary authorities i.e. central banks and finance ministries, as well as securities regulators, a powerful interest in ensuring that the structure and regulation of securities markets and intermediaries reinforce the ability of the system to manage and absorb shocks.

192. This report has considered the scope for such structural improvements under four headings: market mechanisms, settlement and payments systems, supervisory coverage and capital requirements. We conclude that the greatest scope for progress lies in improving settlement systems, and in developing an internationally co-ordinated supervisory system for internationally active intermediaries in securities markets.

193. There is no evidence that any particular market structure is superior to others. There is in any event a trend towards a blurring of distinctions between auction and dealer markets, with each incorporating features of the other. Whatever the type of trading system chosen for an individual market, its actual organisation in terms of transparency of information on the price and size of trades, security of transactions and investor protection will be important factors, alongside liquidity and cost, in evaluating that market and can affect its capacity to identify and contain systemic risks. Intermediaries evidently carry the greatest risk, however, in those markets where they customarily take large positions as principals. In that sense competing market maker structures give rise to greater systemic concern than pure auction markets. But since such structures arguably best suit the requirements of markets in which the main investors are financial institutions wishing to deal frequently in large size, we do not see this as an argument for dismantling them but as one for focusing attention on the risk management of the intermediaries.

194. This does not mean that exchange and other market authorities have no scope to make useful improvements to market mechanisms. In particular, measures to expand capacity of the kind already introduced by the New York Stock Exchange and others should be helpful in handling abnormal volumes of business. Similarly, further development of automated trading may be helpful in handling order flow and in improving information on exposures. But doubts remain about the capacity of automated systems to handle lumpy order flows. In extreme conditions any system may become overloaded.

195. The curbs on programme trading introduced in the United States and the bill proposing to give the SEC powers to regulate such trading can be seen in this context as measures to deal with abnormal conditions. We do not, however, see the proscription of particular trading techniques as a lasting contribution to systemic protection.

196. Similarly, circuit breakers of one form or another only come into play when a disorderly market has arisen. They can be helpful in moderating that disorder, by giving a pause for reflection and reaction by investors, intermediaries and regulators. But as much care needs to be given to devising a satisfactory mechanism for restarting as for closing markets. To be fully effective, trading halts have to be co-ordinated between securities and derivative markets, and even if this is done within one country there remains the problem of dealing outside the exchanges and outside the country. Circuit breakers cannot ensure that, once trading reopens, panic will not revive. Their availability cannot guarantee the containment of systemic contagion in a major market crisis.

197. Settlement arrangements can be an independent source of systemic risk -- through computer breakdown, or through concentration of risk in a clearing house inadequate to sustain it in a crisis, or because incompatibility between timetables and legal obligations in different but related markets increases the strains on users as turnover rises at a time of market disturbance; strains which may begin as liquidity and turn into solvency problems. Moreover they are, by definition, the channel through which counterparty risk is crystallised and transmitted. Organised settlement systems thus offer the opportunity to reduce or redistribute risks in a way which provides better protection for participants in the markets and for the system as a whole.

198. Recent reports by the Group of Thirty, the FIBV, ISSA and Dr. Kessler have made various recommendations for improving and accelerating settlement arrangements within and between national securities markets. We strongly endorse the main thrust of these recommendations -- to move to shorter settlement periods, rolling settlement, book entry transfer systems, and links between settlement arrangements in home and host countries; and, above all, to achieve simultaneous good delivery of securities against payment for them.

199. These goals may take a long time to reach. Legal problems as well as technological and cost factors will have to be overcome. In the meantime, and in the process of resolving them, there are various ways in which risks can be better exposed and managed, as discussed in Section F of this report. The optimal combination of such measures will vary from country to country according to its own legal and market environment. But, in general, it appears that the greatest contributions to the management of risk can potentially come from the achievement of delivery versus payment, shortening of settlement periods, and the construction of legally valid systems of netting, probably involving the use of central counterparties.

200. Since, however, the interposition of a central counterparty itself concentrates risk, arrangements to ensure its financial integrity then become critical. In this respect the arrangements for setting and for collecting margins from clearing members are particularly important. Margin requirements in futures markets are normally determined by the clearing organisations linked to individual exchanges, rather than by national regulators. We have some concern that in striking a balance between market liquidity and prudential considerations, they may, in a competitive environment, attach too much weight to liquidity. Paradoxically, this may lead them into the position where they need to increase margin requirements sharply in a crisis, so adding to the liquidity stresses already developing. We believe that national regulatory authorities should monitor more closely the initial and maintenance margin requirements set by clearing houses and, where necessary, encourage them to increase the degree of protection which they provide against the possibility of extreme price movements.

201. There are large variations between different national régimes for supervision of securities business; in their institutional and functional coverage, in the status of supervisory authorities, and in the number of authorities within countries. These reflect differences in market structure, in stages of development, and in constraints on the types of activity which particular kinds of intermediary are

permitted to perform (such as the laws in the United States and Japan which enforce separation of commercial banking from investment business).

202. This diversity in regulatory coverage causes international systemic concern because it encourages regulatory arbitrage, leaves some significant risk-taking activities by intermediaries outside the supervisory net, fails to deliver a comprehensive supervisory oversight of conglomerates, and complicates the task of international co-operation between supervisory authorities.

203. The existence of non-regulated entities within groups, particularly in the case of the major United States non-bank securities houses, constitutes the most critical gap in coverage. The collapse of Drexel Burnham Lambert reinforces the case, from an international as well as an American standpoint, for the enactment of the legislative proposals put forward by the SEC enabling them to collect financial information from the affiliates, subsidiaries and holding companies of registered broker-dealers.

204. Where several national and functional regulators supervise different parts of a financial conglomerate, arrangements for exchanges of information between them need to be developed. Current bilateral and multilateral efforts to establish such arrangements, with suitable conditions for access, usage and confidentiality, should be intensified. The personal contacts and trust built up in the process themselves become invaluable when co-ordinated action is required in a crisis.

205. Some members of the group, particularly the SEC representatives, believe that the more thorough development of exchanges of information would be sufficient to achieve an adequate improvement in internationally co-ordinated supervision, and significantly reduce systemic risks. Other members of the group, especially the German representatives, hold that full consolidation by a single supervisor ought to be applied to groups taking both credit and market risks. In between these positions, other members of the group believe that serious consideration needs to be given to the construction of a more closely integrated system of supervision of internationally active intermediaries in securities markets. The latter approach might lead to the recognition by other regulators of a lead regulator in the home country of the conglomerate who would have access to comprehensive information about the operations of the whole group and exercise at least a qualitative form of consolidated supervision over the financial operations within the group. If they wished to achieve this, securities regulators would probably need to develop their equivalent of the Basle Concordat for banking supervisors, defining the respective responsibilities of home and host country supervisors. Because many conglomerates do both banking and securities business, such an exercise would itself need to be co-ordinated with banking supervisors; and it would naturally need to address itself to the supervision of subsidiaries, affiliates and holding companies as well as of branches.

206. The justification for the development in one form or another of such a system of central oversight of internationally active intermediaries would be to reduce systemic risks. It would not and should not imply that the authorities would invariably step in to prevent the failure of any individual firm. The aim would rather be to reinforce best practices in the risk management of such groups and, in so doing, reduce the frequency of occasions when official intervention might be judged necessary.

207. Even without an integrated system of supervision of internationally active securities intermediaries, with no gaps in coverage, convergence in the financial requirements imposed by different regulators is itself a desirable goal, for competitive as well as prudential reasons. Both securities and banking supervisors need to continue their efforts, through Basle, IOSCO and the EC, to achieve greater consistency in setting minimum capital adequacy requirements for position and other risks. Harmonising capital requirements for banks and non-bank securities firms is a formidable task, complicated by differences in the nature of the core business of the two types of institution and in the established approaches of banking and securities supervisors. Some members of the Group believe that this requires

identity of treatment in the requirements imposed on both kinds of institutions, others that broad equivalence would be both appropriate and sufficient. Current international efforts need to continue to be pursued intensively to achieve workable solutions.

208. As with margin requirements in futures markets, there may be a case for supervisors to consider for giving an additional weight to the increased possibility which we see of extreme price movements, in setting the levels of capital requirements for securities intermediaries. This need not mean that capital requirements should be set at prohibitive levels, or should attempt to prevent any intermediary failing. Their main objective would remain to allow an orderly unwinding of positions of a firm or firms in difficulty if that became necessary, but an additional systemic safety margin would be built in to cope with conditions of severe international market disturbance.

209. Although the members of the ad hoc group responsible for this report include officials from some of the main regulatory authorities in the world, the OECD is not itself a regulatory body: nor do we envisage that it should aspire to a co-ordinating role in securities regulation. But the OECD does have a continuing interest in the efficient functioning of free international capital markets. Financial crises -- and at the extreme systemic breakdowns -- disrupt that functioning, weaken confidence in those capital markets, and in some measure undermine the international free market economy of which they are an integral part. That is why the range of issues to do with market structures, settlement systems, regulatory coverage, and financial requirements considered in this report are important. In publishing our conclusions the OECD may, we hope, energise the thinking and the actions of the national and international regulatory bodies, governments and central banks responsible for decisions whether and how to carry them forward.

NOTES

1. E. Dimson and P. Marsh, "Implications of Internationalisation for Portfolio Investment", paper presented at Conference on International Markets and Investment, Institute of Finance and Accounting, London Business School, February 1989.

2. E. Bertero and C. Mayer, "Structure and Performance: Global Interdependence of Stock Markets around the Crash of October 1987", Centre for Economic Policy Research, Discussion Paper No. 307, March 1989.

3. D. Newmark, P.A. Tinsley and S. Tosini, "After-Hours Stock Prices and Post-Crash Hangovers", Finance and Economic Discussion Series, Working Paper No. 50, Federal Reserve Board, Washington D.C., November 1988.

4. M. King, E. Sentana and S. Wadwhani, "Volatility and Links between National Stock Markets", National Bureau of Economic Research, Working Paper No. 3357, 1990.

5. G. Duffee, P. Kupiec and P. White, "A Primer on Program Trading and Stock Price Volatility: A Survey of the issues and the Evidence", Finance and Economic Discussion Series No. 109, Federal Reserve Board, Washington D.C., January 1990.

6. S. Becketti and G.H. Sellon, Jr., "Has Financial Market Volatility Increased?", Economic Review, Federal Reserve Bank of Kansas City, March 1990.

7. "Report of the Presidential Task Force on Market Mechanisms", ("Brady Report"), Washington D.C., January 1988.

8. E.P. Davis, "Instability in the Euromarkets and the Economic Theory of Financial Crisis", Bank of England Discussion Paper No. 43, October 1989.

9. S. O'Connor, Bank of Canada, "Systemic Risk in Securities Markets: A Concept in Search of a Definition", unpublished paper written for the Ad Hoc Group, October 1989.

10. "Quality of Markets Quarterly", Winter 1987/88, The International Stock Exchange, London.

11. "Market Volatility and Investor Confidence", report to the Board of the New York Stock Exchange by a specially appointed Panel, chaired by Roger B. Smith, June 1990.

12. "Trading Analysis of 13th and 16th October 1989", report by the Division of Market Regulation, United States Securities and Exchange Commission, May 1990.

13. "Interim Report of the Working Group on Financial Markets", submitted to the President of the United States, May 1988.

14. R. Cantor, "Price Limits and Volatility in Soybean Meal Futures Markets", Federal Reserve Bank of New York, Research Paper No. 8904, 1989.

15. "Report on Stock Index Futures and Cash Market Activity during October 1989", Staff Report by the Commodity Futures Trading Commission, May 1990.

16. "New Financial Instruments and Financial Futures Markets", report to the Minister of State for the Economy, Finance and Privatisation by a Committee of Investigation chaired by Mr. Daniel Deguen ("Deguen Report"), Paris, March 1988.

17. R.J. Shiller, "Causes of Changing Financial Market Volatility", presented at Symposium on Financial Market Volatility: Causes, Consequences and Policy Responses, Federal Reserve Bank of Kansas City, August 1988.

18. P.H. Kupiec, "Futures Margins and Stock Price Volatility: Is there any link?", Finance and Economic Discussion Series, Working Paper No. 104, Federal Reserve Board, Washington D.C., January 1990.

19. J.R. Kessler, "Risks in the Clearing and Settlement Systems of Markets for Financial Futures and Options", commissioned by and presented to the OECD, to be published.

20. See note 7 above.

21. "Interim Report on Stock Index Futures and Cash Market Activity during 1987", November 1987, and "Follow-Up Report on Financial Oversight of Stock Index Futures Markets during 1987", January 1988, by the Commodity Futures Trading Commission.

22. See note 13 above.

23. "The October 1987 Market Break", report by the Division of Market Regulation, United States Securities and Exchange Commission, February 1988.

24. See note 21 above.

25. See note 13 above.

26. "ISSA 4 -- Symposium Report", including twelve recommendations on settlement and clearing processes reached at the fourth symposium of the International Society of Securities Administrators (ISSA), Switzerland, May 1988.

27. J.R. Kessler, "Study on Improvements in the Settlement of Cross-Border Securities Transactions in the European Economic Community", Study for the Commission of the European Economic Community, Directorate- General XV, Financial Institutions and Company Law, July 1988.

28. "Clearance and Settlement Systems in the World's Securities Markets", report by the Group of Thirty, New York and London, March 1989.

29. "Improving International Settlements", report by the task force, chaired by Mr. Jeffrey Knight, appointed by the Féderation Internationale des Bourses de Valeurs (FIBV), June 1989.

30. "Report on Netting Schemes", prepared by the Group of Experts on Payment Systems of the Central Banks of the Group of Ten Countries, Basle, February 1989.

31. "Global Capital Markets 1989", a survey by Klynweld Peat Marwick Goerdeler (KPMG), International Office, Amsterdam, published as a Euromoney Special Report, October 1989.

32. G.E. Corrigan, President, Federal Reserve Bank of New York, Speech to the New York State Bankers Association, January 1990.

33. "International Convergence of Capital Measurement and Capital Standards", issued by the Basle Committee on Banking Regulations and Supervisory Practices, July 1988.

34. "Capital Adequacy Standards for Securities Firms", report of the Technical Committee of the International Organisation of Securities Commissions (IOSCO), August 1989.

Annex I

MEMBERS OF THE OECD AD HOC GROUP OF EXPERTS ON SECURITIES MARKETS

CHAIRMAN

Mr. M.E. Hewitt
Bank of England

* * * * * *

AUSTRALIA

Mr. F. Campbell
Reserve Bank of Australia

Mr. K.M. Hall
Reserve Bank of Australia

AUSTRIA

Mr. A. Gancz
Bundesministerium für Finanzen

Mr. M. Heider
Vienna Stock Exchange

Mr. V. Kamp
Vienna Stock Exchange

Mrs. A. Mörtl
Bundesministerium für Finanzen

Mr. K. Neuteufel
Vienna Stock Exchange

BELGIUM

Mr. M. Algoet
Caisse de Garantie des Agents de Change

Mr. E.C. Dauw
Commission Bancaire

Mr. M.R. Guillaume
Commission de la Bourse de Bruxelles

Mrs. S. Volmer
Ministère des finances

CANADA

Mr. P. Bergeron
Department of Finance

Ms. P. Evanoff
Department of Finance

Ms. D. Meredith
Department of Finance

Mr. S. O'Connor
Bank of Canada

DENMARK

Mr. N. Bartholdy
Danmarks Nationalbank

Mr. F. Lauritzen
Danmarks Nationalbank

Mr. E.H. Pedersen
Danmarks Nationalbank

FINLAND

Mrs. K. Kallio
Bank of Finland

FRANCE

Mr. D. Davydoff
Commission des Opérations de Bourse

Mr. A. de Salins
Direction du Trésor

Mr. P. Devos
Direction du Trésor

Mr. G. Gardella
Conseil du Marché à Terme

Mr. C. Jimenez
Secrétariat de la Commission Bancaire

Mr. R. Leblanc
Societé des Bourses Françaises

Mrs. S. Matherat
Secrétariat Général de la Commission Bancaire

Mr. J. Peure
Banque de France

Mr. A. Tanti
Direction du Trésor

GERMANY

Mrs. C. Hasche-Preusse
Bundesminsterium der Finanzen

Mr. M. Kiesel
German Delegation to the OECD

Mr. J.R. Kessler
Consultant

GERMANY (contd.)

Mr. D. Klein
Deutsche Bundesbank

Mr. H.U. Lellek
Bundesminsterium der Finanzen

Mr. Uresel
German Delegation to the OECD

GREECE

Mr. K. Liakopoulos
Greek Delegation to the OECD

ITALY

Mr. C. Caranza
Banca d'Italia

Mr. C. Giannini
Banca d'Italia

Ms. C. Rossi
Banca d'Italia

Mr. C. Salini
Commissione Nazionale par le Societa e la Borsa

Mr. G. Zadra
Commissione Nazionale par le Societa e la Borsa

JAPAN

Mr. K. Aramaki
Ministry of Finance

Mr. N. Mori
Ministry of Finance

JAPAN (contd.)

Mr. T. Shikibu
Japanese Delegation to the OECD

Mr. H. Tsuda
Japanese Delegation to the OECD

LUXEMBOURG

Mr. C. Kieffer
Commissaire du Gouvernement auprès de la Bourse du Luxembourg

Mr. S. Kolb
Institut Monétaire Luxembourgeois

NETHERLANDS

Mr. R.T. Harmsen
Netherlands Delegation to the OECD

Mr. R. Soeting
De Nederlandsche Bank

NORWAY

Mr. J. Bjoerland
Ministry of Finance

Mr. K. Hagelund
Bank of Norway

Ms. R. Saether
Norwegian Banking, Insurance and Securities Commission

PORTUGAL

Mr. R. Carlos
Commission for Securities Markets

PORTUGAL (contd.)

Mrs. M.C. Machado
Bank of Portugal

Mr. V. Rapaz
Portuguese Delegation to the OECD

SPAIN

Mrs. C. Fuente
Spanish Delegation to the OECD

Mr. R. Martinez-Pardo
Comision Nacional del Mercado de Valores

Mr. S. Ubiria
Comision Nacional del Mercado de Valores

SWEDEN

Mr. R. Gustavii
Sveriges Riksbank

SWITZERLAND

Mr. M. Baltensperger
Swiss National Bank

Mr. M. Zurlinden
Swiss Delegation to the OECD

TURKEY

Mr. T. Acar
Capital Market Board

Mrs. B. Altintaj
Capital Market Board

TURKEY (contd.)

Mrs. N. Arikel
Turkish Delegation to the OECD

Mr. E. Dikmen
Turkish Delegation to the OECD

Ms. H. Uzeler
Undersecretariat of Treasury and Foreign Trade

UNITED KINGDOM

Mr. T.A. Clark
Bank of England

Mrs. P.D. Jackson
Securities and Investments Board

UNITED STATES

Mr. M.D. Fitterman
Securities and Exchange Commission

Mrs. B. Geiser
United States Delegation to the OECD

Mr. H. Kramer
Securities and Exchange Commission

Mr. H. Melamed
Securities and Exchange Commission

Mr. A. Rodriguez
United States Delegation to the OECD

Mrs. M. Scanlon
Federal Reserve Board

Mr. T. Simpson
Federal Reserve Board

BIS

Mr. C. Borio

Mr. C. Butler

EC

Mr. V. Andres Maldonado

Mr. J.M. Fombellida Prieto

Mr. J. Pessoa Costa

IMF

Mr. M. El-Erian

Mr. M. Allen

Mr. D. Folkerts Landau

Mr. Y. Harada

OECD SECRETARIAT

Mr. G. Bröker

Mr. J. Schuijer

Mr. N. Hashimoto

WHERE TO OBTAIN OECD PUBLICATIONS – OÙ OBTENIR LES PUBLICATIONS DE L'OCDE

Argentina – Argentine
CARLOS HIRSCH S.R.L.
Galería Güemes, Florida 165, 4° Piso
1333 Buenos Aires Tel. 30.7122, 331.1787 y 331.2391
Telegram: Hirsch-Baires
Telex: 21112 UAPE-AR. Ref. s/2901
Telefax:(1)331-1787

Australia – Australie
D.A. Book (Aust.) Pty. Ltd.
648 Whitehorse Road, P.O.B 163
Mitcham, Victoria 3132 Tel. (03)873.4411
Telefax: (03)873.5679

Austria – Autriche
OECD Publications and Information Centre
Schedestrasse 7
D-W 5300 Bonn 1 (Germany) Tel. (49.228)21.60.45
Telefax: (49.228)26.11.04

Gerold & Co.
Graben 31
Wien I Tel. (0222)533.50.14

Belgium – Belgique
Jean De Lannoy
Avenue du Roi 202
B-1060 Bruxelles Tel. (02)538.51.69/538.08.41
Telex: 63220 Telefax: (02) 538.08.41

Canada
Renouf Publishing Company Ltd.
1294 Algoma Road
Ottawa, ON K1B 3W8 Tel. (613)741.4333
Telex: 053-4783 Telefax: (613)741.5439
Stores:
61 Sparks Street
Ottawa, ON K1P 5R1 Tel. (613)238.8985
211 Yonge Street
Toronto, ON M5B 1M4 Tel. (416)363.3171

Federal Publications
165 University Avenue
Toronto, ON M5H 3B8 Tel. (416)581.1552
Telefax: (416)581.1743
Les Publications Fédérales
1185 rue de l'Université
Montréal, PQ H3B 3A7 Tel.(514)954-1633

Les Éditions La Liberté Inc.
3020 Chemin Sainte-Foy
Sainte-Foy, PQ G1X 3V6 Tel. (418)658.3763
Telefax: (418)658.3763

Denmark – Danemark
Munksgaard Export and Subscription Service
35, Nørre Søgade, P.O. Box 2148
DK-1016 København K Tel. (45 33)12.85.70
Telex: 19431 MUNKS DK Telefax: (45 33)12.93.87

Finland – Finlande
Akateeminen Kirjakauppa
Keskuskatu 1, P.O. Box 128
00100 Helsinki Tel. (358 0)12141
Telex: 125080 Telefax: (358 0)121.4441

France
OECD/OCDE
Mail Orders/Commandes par correspondance:
2, rue André-Pascal
75775 Paris Cédex 16 Tel. (33-1)45.24.82.00
Bookshop/Librairie:
33, rue Octave-Feuillet
75016 Paris Tel. (33-1)45.24.81.67
(33-1)45.24.81.81

Telex: 620 160 OCDE
Telefax: (33-1)45.24.85.00 (33-1)45.24.81.76

Librairie de l'Université
12a, rue Nazareth
13100 Aix-en-Provence Tel. 42.26.18.08
Telefax : 42.26.63.26

Germany – Allemagne
OECD Publications and Information Centre
Schedestrasse 7
D-W 5300 Bonn 1 Tel. (0228)21.60.45
Telefax: (0228)26.11.04

Greece – Grèce
Librairie Kauffmann
28 rue du Stade
105 64 Athens Tel. 322.21.60
Telex: 218187 LIKA Gr

Hong Kong
Swindon Book Co. Ltd.
13 - 15 Lock Road
Kowloon, Hong Kong Tel. 366.80.31
Telex: 50 441 SWIN HX Telefax: 739.49.75

Iceland – Islande
Mál Mog Menning
Laugavegi 18, Pósthólf 392
121 Reykjavik Tel. 15199/24240

India – Inde
Oxford Book and Stationery Co.
Scindia House
New Delhi 110001 Tel. 331.5896/5308
Telex: 31 61990 AM IN
Telefax: (11)332.5993
17 Park Street
Calcutta 700016 Tel. 240832

Indonesia – Indonésie
Pdii-Lipi
P.O. Box 269/JKSMG/88
Jakarta 12790 Tel. 583467
Telex: 62 875

Ireland – Irlande
TDC Publishers – Library Suppliers
12 North Frederick Street
Dublin 1 Tel. 744835/749677
Telex: 33530 TDCP EI Telefax: 748416

Italy – Italie
Libreria Commissionaria Sansoni
Via Benedetto Fortini, 120/10
Casella Post. 552
50125 Firenze Tel. (055)64.54.15
Telex: 570466 Telefax: (055)64.12.57
Via Bartolini 29
20155 Milano Tel. 36.50.83
La diffusione delle pubblicazioni OCSE viene assicurata dalle principali librerie ed anche da:
Editrice e Libreria Herder
Piazza Montecitorio 120
00186 Roma Tel. 679.46.28
Telex: NATEL I 621427

Libreria Hoepli
Via Hoepli 5
20121 Milano Tel. 86.54.46
Telex: 31.33.95 Telefax: (02)805.28.86

Libreria Scientifica
Dott. Lucio de Biasio 'Aeiou'
Via Meravigli 16
20123 Milano Tel. 805.68.98
Telefax: 800175

Japan – Japon
OECD Publications and Information Centre
Landic Akasaka Building
2-3-4 Akasaka, Minato-ku
Tokyo 107 Tel. (81.3)3586.2016
Telefax: (81.3)3584.7929

Korea – Corée
Kyobo Book Centre Co. Ltd.
P.O. Box 1658, Kwang Hwa Moon
Seoul Tel. (REP)730.78.91
Telefax: 735.0030

Malaysia/Singapore – Malaisie/Singapour
Co-operative Bookshop Ltd.
University of Malaya
P.O. Box 1127, Jalan Pantai Baru
59700 Kuala Lumpur
Malaysia Tel. 756.5000/756.5425
Telefax: 757.3661

Information Publications Pte. Ltd.
Pei-Fu Industrial Building
24 New Industrial Road No. 02-06
Singapore 1953 Tel. 283.1786/283.1798
Telefax: 284.8875

Netherlands – Pays-Bas
SDU Uitgeverij
Christoffel Plantijnstraat 2
Postbus 20014
2500 EA's Gravenhage Tel. (070 3)78.99.11
Voor bestellingen: Tel. (070 3)78.98.80
Telex: 32486 stdru Telefax: (070 3)47.63.51

New Zealand – Nouvelle-Zélande
GP Publications Ltd.
Customer Services
33 The Esplanade - P.O. Box 38-900
Petone, Wellington
Tel. (04)685-555 Telefax: (04)685-333

Norway – Norvège
Narvesen Info Center - NIC
Bertrand Narvesens vei 2
P.O. Box 6125 Etterstad
0602 Oslo 6 Tel. (02)57.33.00
Telex: 79668 NIC N Telefax: (02)68.19.01

Pakistan
Mirza Book Agency
65 Shahrah Quaid-E-Azam
Lahore 3 Tel. 66839
Telex: 44886 UBL PK. Attn: MIRZA BK

Portugal
Livraria Portugal
Rua do Carmo 70-74, Apart. 2681
1117 Lisboa Codex Tel.: 347.49.82/3/4/5
Telefax: (01) 347.02.64

Singapore/Malaysia – Singapour/Malaisie
See "Malaysia/Singapore" – Voir «Malaisie/Singapour»

Spain – Espagne
Mundi-Prensa Libros S.A.
Castelló 37, Apartado 1223
Madrid 28001 Tel. (91) 431.33.99
Telex: 49370 MPLI Telefax: 575.39.98

Libreria Internacional AEDOS
Consejo de Ciento 391
08009 - Barcelona Tel. (93) 301-86-15
Telefax: (93) 317-01-41

Llibreria de la Generalitat
Palau Moja, Rambla dels Estudis, 118
08002 - Barcelona Telefax: (93) 412.18.54
Tel. (93) 318.80.12 (Subscripcions)
(93) 302.67.23 (Publicacions)

Sri Lanka
Centre for Policy Research
c/o Mercantile Credit Ltd.
55, Janadhipathi Mawatha
Colombo 1 Tel. 438471-9, 440346
Telex: 21138 VAVALEX CE Telefax: 94.1.448900

Sweden – Suède
Fritzes Fackboksföretaget
Box 16356, Regeringsgatan 12
103 27 Stockholm Tel. (08)23.89.00
Telex: 12387 Telefax: (08)20.50.21

Subscription Agency/Abonnements:
Wennergren-Williams AB
Nordenflychtsvägen 74, Box 30004
104 25 Stockholm Tel. (08)13.67.00
Telex: 19937 Telefax: (08)618.62.32

Switzerland – Suisse
OECD Publications and Information Centre
Schedestrasse 7
D-W 5300 Bonn 1 (Germany) Tel. (49.228)21.60.45
Telefax: (49.228)26.11.04

Librairie Payot
6 rue Grenus
1211 Genève 11 Tel. (022)731.89.50
Telex: 28356
Subscription Agency – Service des Abonnements
Naville S.A.
7, rue Lévrier
1201 Genève Tél.: (022) 732.24.00
Telefax: (022) 738.48.03

Maditec S.A.
Chemin des Palettes 4
1020 Renens/Lausanne Tel. (021)635.08.65
Telefax: (021)635.07.80

United Nations Bookshop/Librairie des Nations-Unies
Palais des Nations
1211 Genève 10 Tel. (022)734.14.73
Telex: 412962 Telefax: (022)740.09.31

Taiwan – Formose
Good Faith Worldwide Int'l. Co. Ltd.
9th Floor, No. 118, Sec. 2
Chung Hsiao E. Road
Taipei Tel. 391.7396/391.7397
Telefax: (02) 394.9176

Thailand – Thaïlande
Suksit Siam Co. Ltd.
1715 Rama IV Road, Samyan
Bangkok 5 Tel. 251.1630

Turkey – Turquie
Kültur Yayinlari Is-Türk Ltd. Sti.
Atatürk Bulvari No. 191/Kat. 21
Kavaklidere/Ankara Tel. 25.07.60
Dolmabahce Cad. No. 29
Besiktas/Istanbul Tel. 160.71.88
Telex: 43482B

United Kingdom – Royaume-Uni
HMSO
Gen. enquiries Tel. (071) 873 0011
Postal orders only:
P.O. Box 276, London SW8 5DT
Personal Callers HMSO Bookshop
49 High Holborn, London WC1V 6HB
Telex: 297138 Telefax: 071 873 2000
Branches at: Belfast, Birmingham, Bristol, Edinburgh, Manchester

United States – États-Unis
OECD Publications and Information Centre
2001 L Street N.W., Suite 700
Washington, D.C. 20036-4910 Tel. (202)785.6323
Telefax: (202)785.0350

Venezuela
Libreria del Este
Avda F. Miranda 52, Aptdo. 60337, Edificio Galipán
Caracas 106 Tel. 951.1705/951.2307/951.1297
Telegram: Libreste Caracas

Yugoslavia – Yougoslavie
Jugoslovenska Knjiga
Knez Mihajlova 2, P.O. Box 36
Beograd Tel.: (011)621.992
Telex: 12466 jk bgd Telefax: (011)625.970

Orders and inquiries from countries where Distributors have not yet been appointed should be sent to: OECD Publications Service, 2 rue André-Pascal, 75775 Paris Cedex 16, France.

Les commandes provenant de pays où l'OCDE n'a pas encore désigné de distributeur devraient être adressées à : OCDE, Service des Publications, 2, rue André-Pascal, 75775 Paris Cédex 16, France.

75880–7/91

OECD PUBLICATIONS, 2, rue André-Pascal, 75775 PARIS CEDEX 16
PRINTED IN FRANCE
(21 91 01 1) ISBN 92-64-13454-9 - No. 45461 1991